CHANT AND BE HAPPY

THE POWER OF MANTRA MEDITATION

BASED ON THE TEACHINGS OF
HIS DIVINE GRACE
A.C. BHAKTIVEDANTA SWAMI PRABHUPĀDA
Founder-*Ācārya* of the International Society for Krishna Consciousness

THE BHAKTIVEDANTA BOOK TRUST
Los Angeles · London · Paris · Bombay · Sydney · Hong Kong

Readers interested in the subject matter of this book are invited by the International Society for Krishna Consciousness to visit any ISKCON center (see address list in back of book) or to correspond with the secretary.

Telephone: 1-800-927-4152
http://www.harekrishna.com/ara
e-mail: letters@harekrishna.com

International Society for Krishna Consciousness
3764 Watseka Avenue
Los Angeles, CA 90034
USA

International Society for Krishna Consciousness
P.O. Box 324 Borehamwood, Herts.
WD6 1NB, U.K.

International Society for Krishna Consciousness
P.O. Box 262
Botany, NSW 2019
Australia

Text: Drutakarmā dāsa (Michael A. Cremo), Mukunda Goswami, Bhūtātmā dāsa (Austin Gordon), and Mahārudra dāsa (Jeff Long)

Art: Locana dāsa, Parīkṣit dāsa, Muralīdhara dāsa, Śrīnivāsa dāsa (black-and-white drawings), Rāmaprasāda dāsa (lettering, p. 62)

Cover design: Rohiṇīpriya dāsa

Fifth Printing, 1999: 80,000
Previous Printings, 1,500,000

Printed in Australia by McPherson's Printing Group

ISBN: 0-89213-118-7

Dedication

We dedicate this book to our beloved spiritual master and guide, His Divine Grace A. C. Bhaktivedanta Swami Prabhupāda, who brought the transcendental teachings of Lord Kṛṣṇa, including the authorized science of reincarnation, to the Western world.

—The Editors

Contemporary Vedic Library Series

The Bhaktivedanta Book Trust Contemporary Vedic Library Series explores subjects of current interest from the perspective of the timeless knowledge of India's Vedic wisdom.

His Divine Grace A. C. Bhaktivedanta Swami Prabhupāda, founder-*ācārya* (spiritual master) of the International Society for Krishna Consciousness, established the Bhaktivedanta Book Trust in 1970 to present Vedic literatures, as received through the authorized disciplic succession, to the people of the modern age. For the first time in history, through Śrīla Prabhupāda's translations and commentaries, the world's most profound philosophical tradition soon began to have a major impact upon a widespread Western audience. Hundreds of scholars worldwide have reviewed Śrīla Prabhupāda's books, acclaiming his consummate erudition and devotion to the original Sanskrit texts, as well as his unique ability to communicate the most profound and subtle philosophical subjects in a simple and easy-to-understand manner. The Encyclopaedia Britannica reported that his voluminous translations from the original Sanskrit and his lucid commentaries "have astounded literary and academic communities worldwide."

Vedic knowledge has been a source of inner peace, profound wisdom, and spiritual inspiration for millions of people since the dawn of time. The Contemporary Vedic Library editions have been designed to demonstrate practically how this transcendental knowledge, when properly applied, will become a key factor in surmounting the myriad problems facing humanity as we enter the twenty-first century.

Contents

Words from George Harrison

Everybody is looking for KṚṢṆA.
Some don't realize that they are, but they are.
KṚṢṆA is GOD, the Source of all that exists,
the Cause of all that is, was, or ever will be.
As GOD is unlimited, HE has many Names.
Allah-Buddha-Jehova-Rāma:
All are KṚṢṆA, all are ONE.
By serving GOD through each thought, word, and
DEED, and by chanting of HIS Holy Names,
the devotee quickly develops God-consciousness.
By chanting

Hare Kṛṣṇa, Hare Kṛṣṇa
Kṛṣṇa Kṛṣṇa, Hare Hare
Hare Rāma, Hare Rāma
Rāma Rāma, Hare Hare

one inevitably arrives at KṚṢṆA Consciousness.
(The proof of the pudding is in the eating!)

ALL YOU NEED IS LOVE (KRISHNA) HARI BOL
George Harrison

Preface

The Search for Happiness

Everyone wants to be happy. Some of us seek happiness through our families, in natural and healthy living, in successful careers, active social lives, fine gourmet foods, gambling, or through sports and exercise. Others experience happiness in politics, the arts, academia, or in hobbies ranging from mechanics and computer science to drama, philanthropy, welfare work, and literally thousands of other activities that comprise man's unending quest for pleasure. Millions of people find their happiness in liquor, mood elevators, tranquilizers, or other drugs.

Each day doctors and scientists discover more about how the human mind and body work. Yet with this abundance of scientific knowledge and space-age technology, which vastly outstrips that of all previous generations, is modern man really any happier than his predecessors?

The basic problem in our search for happiness is that our sources of pleasure are all limited. What many people consider man's most basic and fundamental pleasures—eating and sex—can only occupy a few moments of each day. Our bodies constantly thwart our plans for enjoyment. After all, you can only eat so much before becoming ill. Even sex has its limits.

Chant and Be Happy provides information about how we can expand our pleasure beyond our present limitations. It deals with a pleasure principle that operates beyond the bounds of time and space and emanates from the very innermost part of our being. This book thoroughly explains how this inner happiness can be experienced immediately by anyone, through the mystical power of transcendental sound vibrations.

This technique for obtaining unlimited happiness does not depend on new products touted by Madison Avenue whiz kids or Hollywood moguls, but has been successfully practiced by countless people throughout the ages. *Chant and Be Happy* explains how to use these transcendental sound vibrations to attain the ultimate state of happiness. It's an easy process and it's free.

To achieve this unlimited and imperishable happiness one need only chant and hear what sages of ancient India have for millennia called the Great Chant for Deliverance, the Hare Kṛṣṇa *mahā-mantra.* This simple sixteen-word *mantra* is comprised of sound vibrations powerful enough to awaken the natural happiness within everyone.

Hare Kṛṣṇa, Hare Kṛṣṇa, Kṛṣṇa Kṛṣṇa, Hare Hare
Hare Rāma, Hare Rāma, Rāma Rāma, Hare Hare

In recent years, millions have learned how to chant the Hare Kṛṣṇa *mantra* and experience this true, spiritual happiness. It is the most popular *mantra* in India, the homeland of meditation, and differs from other systems in two ways. First, the complete *mantra* is chanted (not just a fragment of a *mantra*) and, second, the *mantra* is chanted aloud (not silently).

A brief introduction by His Divine Grace A. C. Bhaktivedanta Swami Prabhupāda, the founder-*ācārya* (spiritual master) of the International Society for Krishna Consciousness, explains the exact nature and meaning of the *mantra.* Chapter One, a recent exclusive interview with former Beatle George Harrison, reveals how the Hare Kṛṣṇa *mantra* has played a leading role in his life over the last fifteen years. George explains that although he had achieved riches and fame beyond what most people could ever hope for, he found that there was "nothing higher" than the happiness he experienced from chanting Hare Kṛṣṇa. George discusses his confidence in the *mantra's* powers over death, explains how much of his musical career has been influenced by and intimately connected with the Hare Kṛṣṇa *mantra,* and describes the knowledge, bliss, and spiritual intelligence that comes from chanting.

In Chapter Two, Śrīla Prabhupāda speaks with John Lennon, Yoko Ono, and George Harrison at John's estate in Tittenhurst Park, discussing the potency of the Hare Kṛṣṇa *mantra* as the path to peace and liberation.

Chapter Three is a fascinating account of how Śrīla Prabhupāda brought the chanting of Hare Kṛṣṇa from India to the Western world in the midst of the countercultural turmoil of the 60s and convinced the disillusioned hippies of New York's Greenwich Village and San Francisco's Haight-Ashbury that this *mantra,* not psychedelics and antiwar protests, would make them happy. The history of chanting and meditating for higher consciousness is discussed in Chapter Four. The next chapter delineates the life and teachings of Śrī Caitanya Mahāprabhu, the sixteenth-century saint, mystic, and incarnation of Lord Kṛṣṇa who popularized the timeless practice of chanting the Hare Kṛṣṇa *mantra.*

Chapter Six, a narration taken from one of India's most important historical and philosophical literatures, the *Śrī Caitanya-caritāmṛta,* reveals how by simply hearing the chanting of Hare Kṛṣṇa from a genuine spiritual master anyone's character can be freed from all unwanted qualities.

The next chapter forms a treatise on self-realization, *mantras,* religion, and the power of the mind in meditation, compiled from the teachings presented in Śrīla Prabhupāda's books. Chapter Eight explains the wide-ranging effects and personal benefits one can expect from chanting Hare Kṛṣṇa. The final chapter gives practical, step-by-step instructions for chanting, which if followed will open the door to ultimate happiness.

Introduction

On Chanting

Brought to the West in 1965 by His Divine Grace A. C. Bhaktivedanta Swami Prabhupāda, "Hare Kṛṣṇa" quickly became a household word. In 1979, Dr. A. L. Basham, the world's leading authority on Indian history and religion, wrote of the Hare Kṛṣṇa movement, "It arose out of nothing in less than 20 years and has become known all over the West. This, I feel, is a sign of the times and an important fact in the history of the Western world."

But what exactly do the words "Hare Kṛṣṇa" mean? In this short essay from the LP Krishna Consciousness, *which first introduced Beatles George Harrison and John Lennon to the chanting, Śrīla Prabhupāda explains the meaning of the Hare Kṛṣṇa* mantra.

The transcendental vibration established by the chanting of Hare Kṛṣṇa, Hare Kṛṣṇa, Kṛṣṇa Kṛṣṇa, Hare Hare/ Hare Rāma, Hare Rāma, Rāma Rāma, Hare Hare [Huh-ray; Krish-na; Rahm-uh] is the sublime method for reviving our transcendental consciousness.

As living spiritual souls, we are all originally Kṛṣṇa conscious entities, but due to our association with matter from time immemorial, our consciousness is now adulterated by the material atmosphere. The material atmosphere, in which we are now living, is called *māyā,* or illusion. *Māyā* means "that which is not." And what is this illusion? The illusion is that we are all trying to be lords of material nature, while actually we are under the grip of her stringent laws. When a servant artificially tries to imitate the all-powerful master, he is said to be in illusion. We are trying to exploit the resources of material nature, but actually we are becoming more and more entangled in her complexities. Therefore, although we are engaged in a hard struggle to conquer nature, we are ever more dependent on her. This illusory struggle against material nature can be stopped at once by revival of our eternal Kṛṣṇa consciousness.

Hare Kṛṣṇa, Hare Kṛṣṇa, Kṛṣṇa Kṛṣṇa, Hare Hare is the transcendental process for reviving this original, pure consciousness. By chanting this transcendental vibration, we can cleanse away all misgivings within our hearts. The basic principle of all such misgivings is the false consciousness that I am the lord of all I survey.

Kṛṣṇa consciousness is not an artificial imposition on the mind. This consciousness is the original, natural energy of the living entity. When we hear this transcendental vibration, this consciousness is revived. This simplest method of meditation is recommended for this age. By practical experience also, one can perceive that by chanting this *mahā-mantra,* or the Great Chanting for Deliverance, one can at once feel a transcendental ecstasy coming through from the spiritual stratum.

In the material concept of life we are busy in the matter of sense gratification, as if we were in the lower, animal stage. A little elevated from this status of sense gratification, one is engaged in mental speculation for the purpose of getting out of the material clutches. A little elevated from this speculative status, when one is intelligent enough, one tries to find out the supreme cause of all causes—within and without. And when one is factually on the plane of spiritual understanding, surpassing the stages of sense, mind, and intelligence, he is then on the transcendental plane. This chanting of the Hare Kṛṣṇa *mantra* is enacted from the spiritual platform, and thus this sound vibration surpasses all lower strata of consciousness—namely sensual, mental, and intellectual. There is no need, therefore, to understand the language of the *mantra,* nor is there any need for mental speculation nor any intellectual adjustment for chanting this *mahā-mantra.* It is automatic, coming from the spiritual platform, and as such, anyone can take part in the chanting without any previous qualification. In a more advanced stage, of course, one is not expected to commit offenses on the grounds of spiritual understanding.

But there is no doubt that chanting takes one immediately to the spiritual platform, and one shows the first symptom of this in the urge to dance along with the chanting of the *mantra.* We have seen this practically. Even a child can take part in the chanting and dancing. Of course, for one who is too entangled in material life, it takes a little more time, but even such a materially engrossed man is raised to the spiritual platform very quickly. When the *mantra* is chanted by a pure devotee of the Lord in love, it has the greatest efficacy on hearers, and as such this chanting should be heard from the lips of a pure devotee of the Lord, so that immediate effects can be achieved.

The word *Harā* is the form of addressing the energy of the Lord, and the words *Kṛṣṇa* and *Rāma* are forms of addressing the Lord Himself. Both *Kṛṣṇa* and *Rāma* mean "the supreme pleasure," and *Harā* is the supreme pleasure energy of the Lord, changed to *Hare* in the vocative. The supreme pleasure energy of the Lord helps us to reach the Lord.

The material energy, called *māyā,* is also one of the multienergies of the Lord. And we, the living entities, are the marginal energy of the Lord. The living entities are described as superior to material energy. When the superior energy is in contact with the inferior energy, an incompatible situation arises; but when the superior marginal energy is in contact with the superior energy, Harā, it is established in its happy, normal condition.

These three words, namely *Hare, Kṛṣṇa,* and *Rāma,* are the transcendental seeds of the *mahā-mantra.* The chanting is a spiritual call for the Lord and His energy to give protection to the conditioned soul. This chanting is exactly like the genuine cry of a child for its mother. Mother Hara helps the devotee achieve the Supreme Father's grace, and the Lord reveals Himself to the devotee who chants this *mantra* sincerely.

No other means of spiritual realization is as effective in this age of quarrel and hypocrisy as the chanting of the *mahā-mantra:*

Hare Kṛṣṇa, Hare Kṛṣṇa,
Kṛṣṇa Kṛṣṇa, Hare Hare,
Hare Rāma, Hare Rāma,
Rāma Rāma, Hare Hare.

(For addresses see last pages)

Courtesy Keystone Press

George Harrison chants Hare Kṛṣṇa with London devotees on the rooftop of the Beatles' recording company, Apple Corps. Ltd., London.

1

The Hare Kṛṣṇa *Mantra:* "There's Nothing Higher..."

A 1982 Interview with George Harrison

If you open up your heart
You will know what I mean
We've been polluted so long
But here's a way for you to get clean

By chanting the names of the Lord and
you'll be free
The Lord is awaiting on you all to awaken
and see.
—"Awaiting On You All"
from the album All things Must Pass

In the summer of 1969, before the dissolution of the most popular music group of all time, George Harrison produced a hit single, "The Hare Krishna Mantra," performed by George and the devotees of the London Rādhā-Kṛṣṇa Temple. Soon after rising to the Top 10 or Top 20 best-selling record charts throughout England, Europe, and parts of Asia, the Hare Kṛṣṇa chant became a household word—especially in England, where the BBC had featured the Hare Kṛṣṇa Chanters, as they were then called, four times on the country's most popular television program, Top of the Pops.

At about the same time, five thousand miles away, several shaven-headed, saffron-robed men and sārī-*clad women sang along with John Lennon and Yoko Ono as they recorded the hit song "Give Peace a Chance" in their room at Montreal's Queen Elizabeth Hotel:*

> John and Yoko, Timmy Leary, Rosemary, Tommy Smothers, Bobby Dylan, Tommy Cooper, Derek Taylor, Norman Mailer, Allen Ginsberg, Hare Krishna, Hare Krishna. All we are saying is give peace a chance.*

The Hare Kṛṣṇa devotees had been visiting with the Lennons for several days, discussing world peace and self-realization. Because of this and other widespread exposure, people all over the world soon began to identify the chanting Hare Kṛṣṇa devotees as harbingers of a more simple, joyful, peaceful way of life.

George Harrison was the impetus for the Beatles' spiritual quest of the sixties, and today the chanting of the Hare Kṛṣṇa mahā-mantra*—Hare Kṛṣṇa, Hare Kṛṣṇa, Kṛṣṇa Kṛṣṇa, Hare Hare/ Hare Rāma, Hare Rāma, Rāma Rāma, Hare Hare—still plays a key role in the former Beatle's life.*

In this conversation with his long-time personal friend Contemporary Vedic Library Series editor Mukunda Goswami, taped at George's home in England on September 4, 1982, George reveals some memorable experiences he has had chanting Hare Kṛṣṇa and describes in detail his deep personal realizations about the chanting. He reveals what factors led him to produce "The Hare Krishna Mantra" record, "My Sweet Lord," and the LPs All Things Must Pass *and* Living in the Material World, *which were all influenced to a great extent by the Hare Kṛṣṇa chanting and philosophy. He speaks lovingly and openly about his association with His Divine Grace A. C. Bhaktivedanta Swami Prabhupāda, founder-*ācārya *(spiritual master) of the Hare Kṛṣṇa movement. In the following inter-*

---

*"Give Peace a Chance," © 1969 Northern Songs, Limited

view George speaks frankly about his personal philosophy regarding the Hare Kṛṣṇa movement, music, yoga, *reincarnation,* karma, *the soul, God, and Christianity. The conversation concludes with his fond remembrances of a visit to the childhood abode of Lord Kṛṣṇa in Vṛndāvana, India, home of the Hare Kṛṣṇa* mantra, *and with George discussing some of his celebrity friends' involvement with the* mantra *now heard and chanted around the world.*

Mukunda Goswami: Oftentimes you speak of yourself as a plainclothes devotee, a closet *yogī* or "closet Kṛṣṇa," and millions of people all over the world have been introduced to the chanting by your songs. But what about you? How did you first come in contact with Kṛṣṇa?
George Harrison: Through my visits to India. So by the time the Hare Kṛṣṇa movement first came to England in 1969, John and I had already gotten ahold of Prabhupāda's first album, *Kṛṣṇa Consciousness*. We had played it a lot and liked it. That was the first time I'd ever heard the chanting of the *mahā-mantra*.
Mukunda: Even though you and John Lennon played Śrīla Prabhupāda's record a lot and had chanted quite a bit on your own, you'd never really met any of the devotees. Yet when Guru dāsa, Śyāmasundara, and I [part of the group of six devotees sent from America to open the first Hare Kṛṣṇa temple in London] first came to England, you co-signed the lease on our first temple in central London, bought the Manor* for us, which has provided a place for literally hundreds of thousands of people to learn about Kṛṣṇa consciousness, and financed the first printing of the book *Kṛṣṇa*. You

---

*Bhaktivedanta Manor, a seventeen-acre estate outside London, purchased by George in 1973 and donated to ISKCON for use as a temple and *yoga-āśrama*.

hadn't really known us for a very long time at all. Wasn't this a kind of sudden change for you?

George: Not really, for I always felt at home with Kṛṣṇa. You see, it was already a part of me. I think it's something that's been with me from my previous birth. Your coming to England and all that was just like another piece of a jigsaw puzzle that was coming together to make a complete picture. It had been slowly fitting together. That's why I responded to you all the way I did when you first came to London. Let's face it. If you're going to have to stand up and be counted, I figured, "I would rather be with these guys than with those other guys over there." It's like that. I mean I'd rather be one of the devotees of God than one of the straight, so-called sane or normal people who just don't understand that man is a spiritual being, that he has a soul. And I felt comfortable with you all, too, kind of like we'd known each other before. It was a pretty natural thing, really.

Mukunda: George, you were a member of the Beatles, undoubtedly the greatest single pop group in music history, one that influenced not only music, but whole generations of young people as well. After the dissolution of the group, you went on to emerge as a solo superstar with albums like *All Things Must Pass,* the country's top selling album for seven weeks in a row, and its hit single "My Sweet Lord," which was number one in America for two months. That was followed by *Living in the Material World,* number one on *Billboard* for five weeks and a million-selling LP. One song on that album, "Give Me Love," was a smash hit for six straight weeks. The concert for Bangladesh with Ringo Starr, Eric Clapton, Bob Dylan, Leon Russell, and Billy Preston was a phenomenal success and, once the LP and concert film were released, would become the single most successful rock benefit project ever. So, you had material success. You'd been everywhere, done everything, yet at the same time you were on a spiritual quest. What was it that really got you started on your spiritual journey?

George: It wasn't until the experience of the sixties really hit. You know, having been successful and meeting everybody we thought worth meeting and finding out they weren't worth meeting, and having had more hit records than everybody else and having done it bigger than everybody else. It was like reaching the top of a wall and then looking over and seeing that there's so much more on the other side. So I felt it was part of my duty to say, "Oh, okay, maybe you are thinking this is all you need—to be rich and famous—but actually it isn't."

Mukunda: George, in your recently published autobiography, *I, Me, Mine,* you said your song "Awaiting on You All" is about *japa-yoga,* or chanting *mantras* on beads. You explained that a *mantra* is "mystical energy encased in a sound structure," and that "each *mantra* contains within its vibrations a certain power." But of all *mantras,* you stated that "the *mahā-mantra* [the Hare Kṛṣṇa *mantra*] has been prescribed as the easiest and surest way for attaining God Realization in this present age." As a practitioner of *japa-yoga,* what realizations have you experienced from chanting?

George: Prabhupāda* told me once that we should just keep chanting all the time, or as much as possible. Once you do that, you realize the benefit. The response that comes from chanting is in the form of bliss, or spiritual happiness, which is a much higher taste than any happiness found here in the material world. That's why I say that the more you do it, the more you don't want to stop, because it feels so nice and peaceful.

---

* His Divine Grace A. C. Bhaktivedanta Swami Prabhupāda, founder-*ācārya* (spiritual master) of the Hare Kṛṣṇa movement.

Mukunda: What is it about the *mantra* that brings about this feeling of peace and happiness?

George: The word *Hare* is the word that calls upon the energy that's around the Lord. If you say the *mantra* enough, you build up an identification with God. God's all happiness, all bliss, and by chanting His names we connect with Him. So it's really a process of actually having a realization of God, which all becomes clear with the expanded state of consciousness that develops when you chant. Like I said in the introduction I wrote for Prabhupāda's *Kṛṣṇa* book some years ago, "If there's a God, I want to see Him. It's pointless to believe in something without proof, and Kṛṣṇa consciousness and meditation are methods where you can actually obtain God perception."

Mukunda: Is it an instantaneous process, or gradual?

George: You don't get it in five minutes. It's something that takes time, but it works because it's a direct process of attaining God and will help us to have pure consciousness and good perception that is above the normal, everyday state of consciousness.

Mukunda: How do you feel after chanting for a long time?

George: In the life I lead, I find that I sometimes have opportunities when I can really get going at it, and the more I do it, I find the harder it is to stop, and I don't want to lose the feeling it gives me.

For example, once I chanted the Hare Kṛṣṇa *mantra* all the way from France to Portugal, nonstop. I drove for about twenty-three hours and chanted all the way. It gets you feeling a bit invincible. The funny thing was that I didn't even know where I was going. I mean I had bought a map, and I knew basically which way I was aiming, but I couldn't speak French, Spanish, or Portuguese. But none of that seemed to matter. You know, once you get chant-

ing, then things start to happen transcendentally.
Mukunda: The *Vedas* inform us that because God is absolute, there is no difference between God the person and His holy name; the name *is* God. When you first started chanting, could you perceive that?
George: It takes a certain amount of time and faith to accept or to realize that there is no difference between Him and His name, to get to the point where you're no longer mystified by where He is. You know, like, "Is He around here?" You realize after some time, "Here He is—right here!" It's a matter of practice. So when I say that "I see God," I don't necessarily mean to say that when I chant I'm seeing Kṛṣṇa in His original form when He came five thousand years ago, dancing across the water, playing His flute. Of course, that would also be nice, and it's quite possible too. When you become real pure by chanting, you *can* actually see God like that, I mean personally. But no doubt you can feel His presence and know that He's there when you're chanting.
Mukunda: Can you think of any incident where you felt God's presence very strongly through chanting?
George: Once I was on an airplane that was in an electric storm. It was hit by lightning three times, and a Boeing 707 went over the top of us, missing by inches. I thought the back end of the plane had blown off. I was on my way from Los Angeles to New York to organize the Bangladesh concert. As soon as the plane began bouncing around, I started chanting Hare Kṛṣṇa, Hare Kṛṣṇa, Kṛṣṇa Kṛṣṇa, Hare Hare/ Hare Rāma, Hare Rāma, Rāma Rāma, Hare Hare. The whole thing went on for about an hour and a half or two hours, the plane dropping hundreds of feet and bouncing all over in the storm, all the lights out and all these explosions, and everybody terrified. I ended up with my feet pressed against the seat in front, my seat belt as tight as it could be, gripping on the thing, and yelling

Hare Kṛṣṇa, Hare Kṛṣṇa, Kṛṣṇa Kṛṣṇa, Hare Hare at the top of my voice. I know for me, the difference between making it and not making it was actually chanting the *mantra.* Peter Sellers also swore that chanting Hare Kṛṣṇa saved him from a plane crash once.

John Lennon and Hare Kṛṣṇa

Mukunda: Did any of the other Beatles chant?
George: Before meeting Prabhupāda and all of you, I had bought that album Prabhupāda did in New York, and John and I listened to it. I remember we sang it for days, John and I, with ukulele banjos, sailing through the Greek Islands chanting Hare Kṛṣṇa. Like six hours we sang, because we couldn't stop once we got going. As soon as we stopped, it was like the lights went out. It went on to the point where our jaws were aching, singing the *mantra* over and over and over and over and over. We felt exalted; it was a very happy time for us.
Mukunda: You know, I saw a video the other day sent to us from Canada, showing John and Yoko Ono recording their hit song "Give Peace a Chance," and about five or six of the devotees were there in John's room at the Queen Elizabeth Hotel in Montreal, singing along and playing cymbals and drums. You know, John and Yoko chanted Hare Kṛṣṇa on that song. That was in May of '69, and just three months later, Śrīla Prabhupāda was John and Yoko's house guest for one month at their estate outside London.

While Prabhupada was there, you, John, and Yoko came to his room one afternoon for a few hours. I think that was the first time you all met him.
George: That's right.
Mukunda: At that point John was a spiritual seeker, and Prabhupada explained the true path to peace and libera-

tion. He talked about the eternality of the soul, *karma,* and reincarnation, which are all elaborately dealt with in the Vedic literatures.* Although John never made Hare Kṛṣṇa a big part of his life, he echoed the philosophy of Kṛṣṇa consciousness in a hit song he wrote just about a year after that conversation, "Instant Karma."

Now what's the difference between chanting Hare Kṛṣṇa and meditation?

George: It's really the same sort of thing as meditation, but I think it has a quicker effect. I mean, even if you put your beads down, you can still say the *mantra* or sing it without actually keeping track on your beads. One of the main differences between silent meditation and chanting is that silent meditation is rather dependent on concentration, but when you chant, it's more of a direct connection with God.

Practical Meditation

Mukunda: The *mahā-mantra* was prescribed for modern times because of the fast-paced nature of things today. Even when people do get into a little quiet place, it's very difficult to calm the mind for very long.

George: That's right. Chanting Hare Kṛṣṇa is a type of meditation that can be practiced even if the mind is in turbulence. You can even be doing it and other things at the same time. That's what's so nice. In my life there's been many times the *mantra* brought things around. It keeps me in tune with reality, and the more you sit in one place and chant, the more incense you offer to Kṛṣṇa in the same room, the more you purify the vibration, the

---

* A vast body of scriptures, including the four *Vedas,* predating the Bible and covering all aspects of spiritual knowledge from the nature of the self, or individual soul, to the Supreme Soul (Śrī Kṛṣṇa) and His kingdom in the spiritual world.

more you can achieve what you're trying to do, which is just trying to remember God, God, God, God, God, as often as possible. And if you're talking to Him with the *mantra,* it certainly helps.

Mukunda: What else helps you to fix your mind on God?

George: Well, just having as many things around me that will remind me of Him, like incense and pictures. Just the other day I was looking at a small picture on the wall of my studio of you, Gurudāsa, and Śyāmasundara, and just seeing all the old devotees made me think of Kṛṣṇa. I guess that's the business of devotees—to make you think of God.

Mukunda: How often do you chant?

George: Whenever I get a chance.

Mukunda: Once you asked Śrīla Prabhupāda about a particular verse he quoted from the *Vedas,* in which it's said that when one chants the holy name of Kṛṣṇa, Kṛṣṇa dances on the tongue and one wishes one had thousands of ears and thousands of mouths with which to better appreciate the holy names of God.

George: Yes. I think he was talking about the realization that there is no difference between Him standing before you and His being present in His name. That's the real beauty of chanting—you directly connect with God. I have no doubt that by saying *Kṛṣṇa* over and over again, He can come and dance on the tongue. The main thing, though, is to keep in touch with God.

Mukunda: So your habit is generally to use the beads when you chant?

George: Oh, yeah. I have my beads. I remember when I first got them, they were just big knobby globs of wood, but now I'm very glad to say that they're smooth from chanting a lot.

Mukunda: Do you generally keep them in the bag when you chant?

George: Yes. I find it's very good to be touching them. It keeps another one of the senses fixed on God. Beads really help in that respect. You know, the frustrating thing about it was in the beginning there was a period when I was heavy into chanting and I had my hand in my bead bag all the time. And I got so tired of people asking me, "Did you hurt your hand, break it or something?" In the end I used to say, "Yeah. Yeah. I had an accident," because it was easier than explaining everything. Using the beads also helps me to release a lot of nervous energy.

Mukunda: Some people say that if everyone on the planet chanted Hare Kṛṣṇa, they wouldn't be able to keep their minds on what they were doing. In other words, if everyone started chanting, some people ask if the whole world wouldn't just grind to a halt. They wonder if people would stop working in factories, for example.

George: No. Chanting doesn't stop you from being creative or productive. It actually helps you concentrate. I think this would make a great sketch for television: imagine all the workers on the Ford assembly line in Detroit, all of them chanting Hare Kṛṣṇa Hare Kṛṣṇa while bolting on the wheels. Now that would be wonderful. It might help out the auto industry, and probably there would be more decent cars too.

Experiencing God Through the Senses

Mukunda: We've talked a lot about *japa,* or personalized chanting, which most chanters engage in. But there's another type, called *kīrtana,* when one chants congregationally, in a temple or on the streets with a group of devotees. *Kīrtana* generally gives a more supercharged effect, like recharging one's spiritual batteries, and it gives others a chance to hear the holy names and become purified.

Actually, I was with Śrīla Prabhupāda when he first began the group chanting in Tompkins Square Park on New York's Lower East Side in 1966. The poet Allen Ginsberg would come and chant with us a lot and would play on his harmonium. A lot of people would come to hear the chanting, then Prabhupāda would give lectures on *Bhagavad-gītā* back at the temple.

George: Yes, going to a temple or chanting with a group of other people—the vibration is that much stronger. Of course, for some people it's easy just to start chanting on their beads in the middle of a crowd, while other people are more comfortable chanting in the temple. But part of Kṛṣṇa consciousness is trying to tune in all the senses of all the people: to experience God through all the senses, not just by experiencing Him on Sunday, through your knees by kneeling on some hard wooden kneeler in the church. But if you visit a temple, you can see pictures of God, you can see the Deity form of the Lord, and you can just hear Him by listening to yourself and others say the *mantra*. It's just a way of realizing that all the senses can be applied toward perceiving God, and it makes it that much more appealing, seeing the pictures, hearing the *mantra*, smelling the incense, flowers, and so on. That's the nice thing about your movement. It incorporates everything—chanting, dancing, philosophy, and *prasādam**. The music and dancing is a serious part of the process too. It's not just something to burn off excess energy.

Mukunda: We've always seen that when we chant in the streets, people are eager to crowd around and listen. A lot of them tap their feet or dance along.

George: It's great, the sound of the *karatālas* [cymbals]. When I hear them from a few blocks away, it's like some

---

* Vegetarian foods that have been spiritualized by offering them to Lord Kṛṣṇa with love and devotion.

magical thing that awakens something in me. Without their really being aware of what's happening, people are being awakened spiritually. Of course, in another sense, in a higher sense, the *kīrtana* is always going on, whether we're hearing it or not.

Now, all over the place in Western cities, the *saṅkīrtana* party has become a common sight. I love to see these *saṅkīrtana* parties, because I love the whole idea of the devotees mixing it up with everybody, giving everybody a chance to remember. I wrote in the *Kṛṣṇa* book introduction, "Everybody is looking for Kṛṣṇa. Some don't realize that they are, but they are. Kṛṣṇa is God . . . and by chanting His Holy Names, the devotee quickly develops God-Consciousness."

Mukunda: You know, Śrīla Prabhupāda often said that after a large number of temples were established, most people would simply begin to take up the chanting of Hare Kṛṣṇa within their own homes, and we're seeing more and more that this is what's happening. Our worldwide congregation is very large—in the millions. The chanting on the streets, the books, and the temples are there to give people a start, to introduce them to the process.

George: I think it's better that it is spreading into the homes now. There are a lot of "closet Kṛṣṇas," you know. There's a lot of people out there who are just waiting, and if it's not today, it will be tomorrow or next week or next year.

Back in the sixties, whatever we were all getting into, we tended to broadcast it as loud as we could. I had had certain realizations and went through a period where I was so thrilled about my discoveries and realizations that I wanted to shout and tell it to everybody. But there's a time to shout it out and a time not to shout it out. A lot of people went underground with their spiritual life in the seventies, but they're out there in little nooks and crannies and in the countryside, people who look and dress straight, insurance salesmen types, but they're really meditators and chanters, closet devotees.

Prabhupāda's movement is doing pretty well. It's growing like wildfire really. How long it will take until we get to a Golden Age where everybody's perfectly in tune with God's will, I don't know; but because of Prabhupāda, Kṛṣṇa consciousness has certainly spread more in the last sixteen years than it has since the sixteenth century, since the time of Lord Caitanya.* The *mantra* has spread more quickly and the movement's gotten bigger and bigger. It would be great if everyone chanted. Everybody would benefit by doing it. No matter how much money you've got, it doesn't necessarily make you happy. You have to find your happiness with the problems you have, not worry too much about them, and chant Hare Kṛṣṇa, Hare Kṛṣṇa, Kṛṣṇa Kṛṣṇa, Hare Hare.

The Hare Kṛṣṇa Record

Mukunda: In 1969 you produced a single called "The Hare Krishna Mantra," which eventually became a hit in many countries. That tune later became a cut on the Rādhā-Kṛṣṇa Temple album, which you also produced on the Apple label and was distributed in America by Capitol Records. A lot of people in the recording business were surprised by this, your producing songs for and singing with the Hare Kṛṣṇas. Why did you do it?

George: Well, it's just all a part of service, isn't it? Spiritual service, in order to try to spread the *mantra* all over the world. Also, to try and give the devotees a wider base and

* The great saint, mystic, and incarnation of Kṛṣṇa who popularized the chanting of Hare Kṛṣṇa and founded the modern-day Hare Kṛṣṇa movement.

a bigger foothold in England and everywhere else.
Mukunda: How did the success of this record of Hare Kṛṣṇa devotees chanting compare with some of the rock musicians you were producing at the time like Jackie Lomax, Splinter, and Billy Preston?
George: It was a different thing. Nothing to do with that really. There was much more reason to do it. There was less commercial potential in it, but it was much more satisfying to do, knowing the possibilities that it was going to create, the connotations it would have just by doing a three-and-a-half-minute *mantra.* That was more fun really than trying to make a pop hit record. It was the feeling of trying to utilize your skills or job to make it into some spiritual service to Kṛṣṇa.
Mukunda: What effect do you think that tune, "The Hare Krishna Mantra," having reached millions and millions of people, has had on the cosmic consciousness of the world?
George: I'd like to think it had some effect. After all, the sound is God.
Mukunda: When Apple, the recording company, called a press conference to promote the record, the media seemed to be shocked to hear you speak about the soul and God being so important.
George: I felt it was important to try and be precise, to tell them and let them know. You know, to come out of the closet and really tell them. Because once you realize something, then you can't pretend you don't know it any more.

I figured this is the space age, with airplanes and everything. If everyone can go around the world on their holidays, there's no reason why a *mantra* can't go a few miles as well. So the idea was to try to spiritually infiltrate society, so to speak. After I got Apple Records committed to you and the record released, and after our big promotion, we saw it was going to become a hit. And one of the greatest things, one of the greatest thrills of my life, actually, was seeing you all on BBC's *Top of the Pops.* I couldn't believe it. It's pretty hard to get on that program, because they only put you on if you come into the Top 20. It was just like a breath of fresh air. My strategy was to keep it to a three-and-a-half-minute version of the *mantra* so they'd play it on the radio, and it worked. I did the harmonium and guitar track for that record at Abbey Road studios before one of the Beatles' sessions and then overdubbed a bass part. I remember Paul McCartney and his wife, Linda, arrived at the studio and enjoyed the *mantra.*

Mukunda: Paul's quite favorable now, you know.

George: That's good. It still sounds like quite a good recording, even after all these years. It was the greatest fun of all, really, to see Kṛṣṇa on *Top of the Pops.*

Mukunda: Shortly after its release, John Lennon told me that they played it at the intermission right before Bob Dylan did the Isle of Wight concert with Jimi Hendrix, the Moody Blues, and Joe Cocker in the summer of '69.

George: They played it while they were getting the stage set up for Bob. It was great. Besides, it was a catchy tune, and the people didn't have to know what it meant in order to enjoy it. I felt very good when I first heard it was doing well.

Mukunda: How did you feel about the record technically, the voices?

George: Yamuna, the lead singer, has a naturally good voice. I liked the way she sang with conviction, and she sang like she'd been singing it a lot before. It didn't sound like the first tune she'd ever sung.

You know, I used to sing the *mantra* long before I met any of the devotees or long before I met Prabhupāda, because I had his first record then for at least two years. When you're open to something it's like being a beacon, and you attract it. From the first time I heard the chanting, it was like a door opened somewhere in my subconscious, maybe from some previous life.

Mukunda: In the lyrics to that song "Awaiting on You All," from the *All Things Must Pass* album, you come right out front and tell people that they can be free from living in the material world by chanting the names of God. What made you do it? What kind of feedback did you get?

George: At that time, nobody was committed to that type of music in the pop world. There was, I felt, a real need for that, so rather than sitting and waiting for somebody else, I decided to do it myself. A lot of times we think, "Well, I agree with you, but I'm not going to actually stand up and be counted. Too risky." Everybody is always trying to keep themselves covered, stay commercial, so I thought, just do it. Nobody else is, and I'm sick of all these young people just boogeying around, wasting their lives, you know. Also, I felt that there were a lot of people out there who would be reached. I still get letters from people saying, "I have been in the Kṛṣṇa temple for three years, and I would have never known about Kṛṣṇa unless you recorded the *All Things Must Pass* album." So I know, by the Lord's grace, I am a small part in the cosmic play.

Mukunda: What about the other Beatles? What did they think about your taking up Kṛṣṇa consciousness? What was their reaction? You'd all been to India by then and were pretty much searching for something spiritual. Śyāmasundara said that once, when he ate lunch with you and the other Beatles, they were all quite respectful.

George: Oh, yeah, well, if the Fab Four didn't get it, that is, if they couldn't deal with shaven-headed Hare Kṛṣṇas, then there would have been no hope! [Laughter.] And the devotees just came to be associated with me, so people stopped thinking, "Hey, what's this?" you know, if somebody in orange, with a shaved head, would appear. They'd say, "Oh, yeah, they're with George."

Mukunda: From the very start, you always felt comfortable around the devotees?
George: The first time I met Śyāmasundara, I liked him. He was my pal. I'd read about Prabhupāda coming from India to Boston on the back of his record, and I knew that Śyāmasundara and all of you were in my age group, and that the only difference, really, was that you'd already joined and I hadn't. I was in a rock band, but I didn't have any fear, because I had seen *dhotīs,* your robes, and the saffron color and shaved heads in India. Kṛṣṇa consciousness was especially good for me because I didn't get the feeling that I'd have to shave my head, move into a temple, and do it full time. So it was a spiritual thing that just fit in with my life-style. I could still be a musician, but I just changed my consciousness, that's all.
Mukunda: You know, the Tudor mansion and estate that you gave us outside London has become one of our largest international centers. How do you feel about the Bhaktivedanta Manor's success in spreading Kṛṣṇa consciousness?
George: Oh, it's great. And it also relates to making the Hare Kṛṣṇa record or whatever my involvements were. Actually, it gives me pleasure, the idea that I was fortunate enough to be able to help at that time. All those songs with spiritual themes were like little plugs—"My Sweet Lord" and the others. And now I know that people are much more respectful and accepting when it comes to seeing the devotees in the streets and all that. It's no longer like something that's coming from left field.

And I've given a lot of Prabhupāda's books to many people, and whether I ever hear from them again or not, it's good to know that they've gotten them, and if they read them, their lives may be changed.
Mukunda: When you come across people who are spiri-

tually inclined but don't have much knowledge, what kind of advice do you give them?

George: I try to tell them my little bit, what my experience is, and give them a choice of things to read and a choice of places to go—like you know, "Go to the temple, try chanting."

Mukunda: In the "Ballad of John and Yoko," John and Yoko rapped the media for the way it can foster a false image of you and perpetuate it. It's taken a lot of time and effort to get them to understand that we are a genuine religion, with scriptures that predate the New Testament by three thousand years. Gradually, though, more people, scholars, philosophers, and theologians, have come around, and today they have a great deal of respect for the ancient Vaiṣṇava* tradition, where the modern-day Kṛṣṇa consciousness movement has its roots.

George: The media is to blame for *everything,* for all the misconceptions about the movement, but in a sense it didn't really matter if they said something good or bad, because Kṛṣṇa consciousness always seemed to transcend that barrier anyway. The fact that the media was letting people know about Kṛṣṇa was good in itself.

Mukunda: Śrīla Prabhupāda always trained us to stick to our principles. He said that the worst thing we could ever do would be to make some sort of compromise or to dilute the philosophy for the sake of cheap popularity. Although many swamis and *yogīs* had come from India to the West, Prabhupāda was the only one with the purity and devotion to establish India's ancient Kṛṣṇa conscious philosophy around the world on its own terms—not watered down, but as it is.

---

* Devotees of Lord Viṣṇu, or Kṛṣṇa, the Supreme Personality of Godhead.

George: That's right. He was a perfect example of what he preached.

Mukunda: How did you feel about financing the first printing of the *Kṛṣṇa* book and writing the introduction?

George: I just felt like it was part of my job, you know. Wherever I go in the world, when I see devotees, I always say "Hare Kṛṣṇa!" to them, and they're always pleased to see me. It's a nice relationship. Whether they really know me personally or not, they feel they know me. And they do, really.

Mukunda: When you did the *Material World* album, you used a photo insert taken from the cover of Prabhupāda's *Bhagavad-gītā* showing Kṛṣṇa and His friend and disciple, Arjuna. Why?

George: Oh, yeah. It said on the album, "From the cover of *Bhagavad-gītā As It Is* by A. C. Bhaktivedanta Swami." It was a promo for you, of course. I wanted to give them all a chance to see Kṛṣṇa, to know about Him. I mean that's the whole idea, isn't it?

Spiritual Food

Mukunda: At lunch today we spoke a little about *prasādam,* vegetarian foods that have been spiritualized by being offered to Kṛṣṇa in the temple. A lot of people have come to Kṛṣṇa consciousness through *prasādam,* especially through our Sunday Feast of Kṛṣṇa at all of our temples around the world. I mean, this process is the only kind of yoga that you can actually practice by eating.

George: Well, we should try to see God in everything, so it helps so much having the food to taste. Let's face it, if God is in everything, why shouldn't you taste Him when you eat? I think that *prasādam* is a very important thing. Kṛṣṇa is God, so He's absolute: His name, His form, *prasādam,* it's all Him. They say the way to a man's heart is through his stomach, so if you can get to a man's spirit soul by eating, and it works, why not do it? There's nothing better than having been chanting and dancing, or just sitting and talking philosophy, and then suddenly the devotees bring out the *prasādam.* It's a blessing from Kṛṣṇa, and it's spiritually important. The idea is that *prasādam's* the sacrament the Christians talk about, only instead of being just a wafer, it's a whole feast, really, and the taste is so nice—it's out of this world. And *prasādam's* a good little hook in this age of commercialism. When people want something extra, or they need to have something special, *prasādam* will hook them in there. It's undoubtedly done a great deal toward getting a lot more people involved in spiritual life. It breaks down prejudices, too. Because they think, "Oh, well, yes, I wouldn't mind a drink of whatever or a bite of that." Then they ask, "What's this?" and "Oh, well, it's *prasādam.*" And they get to learn another aspect of Kṛṣṇa consciousness. Then they say, "It actually tastes quite nice. Have you got another plateful?" I've seen that happen with lots of people, especially older people I've seen at your temples. Maybe they were a little prejudiced, but the next thing you know, they're in love with *prasādam,* and eventually they walk out of the temple thinking, "They're not so bad after all."

Mukunda: The Vedic literatures reveal that *prasādam* conveys spiritual realization, just as chanting does, but in a less obvious or conspicuous way. You make spiritual advancement just by eating it.

George: I'd say from my experience that it definitely works. I've always enjoyed *prasādam* much more when I've been at the temple, or when I've actually been sitting with Prabhupāda, than when somebody's brought it to me. Sometimes you can sit there with *prasādam* and find that three or four hours have gone by and you didn't even know it. *Prasādam* really helped me a lot, because you start to realize "Now I'm tasting Kṛṣṇa." You're conscious suddenly of another aspect of God, understanding that He's this little *samosā.** It's all just a matter of tuning into the spiritual, and *prasādam's* a very real part of it all.

Mukunda: You know, a lot of rock groups like Grateful Dead and Police get *prasādam* backstage before their concerts. They love it. It's a long-standing tradition with us. I remember one time sending *prasādam* to one of the Beatles' recording sessions. And your sister was telling me today that while you were doing the Bangladesh concert, Syāmasundara used to bring you all *prasādam* at the rehearsals.

George: Yes, he's even got a credit on the album sleeve.

Mukunda: What are your favorite kinds of *prasādam,* George?

George: I really like those deep-fried cauliflower things—*pakorās?*†

Mukunda: Yes.

George: And one thing I always liked was *rasamalai* [a milk sweet]. And there's a lot of good drinks as well, fruit juices and *lassī,* the yogurt drinks mixed with fruit, and sometimes with rose water.

Mukunda: Do you remember the time we called the press in London for a big feast when we were promoting "The Hare Krishna Mantra" record? They were pretty surprised, for no one really knew us then for our food. Now, pretty much when people think about us, they still think, "They're the ones chanting and dancing in the streets," but they're connecting us more and more now with *prasādam*—"They're the ones with those free vegetarian dinners."

George: The press were probably thinking, "Oh, we've got

---

* Cauliflower-and-pea-filled pastry deep-fried in clarified butter.

† Cauliflower dipped in batter and deep-fried in clarified butter.

to go and do this now." And then suddenly they find that they're all sitting around and eating a much better Indian take-away than they would ever have at any one of the local spots. They were pretty impressed.

Mukunda: We've served about 150 million plates of *prasādam* so far at the free feasts around the world, what to speak of our restaurants.

George: You ought to have it up outside on billboards like those hamburger places do. You know, like "150 million served." I think it's great. It's a pity you don't have restaurants or temples on all the main streets of every little town and village like those hamburger and fried chicken places. You should put them out of business.

Mukunda: You've been to our London restaurant, Healthy, Wealthy, and Wise?

George: Lots of times. It's good to have these and other restaurants around, where plainclothes devotees serve the food. People slowly realize, " This is one of the best places I've been," and they keep coming back. Then maybe they pick up a little bit of the literature or a pamphlet there and say, "Oh, hey, that was run by the Hare Kṛṣṇas." I think there's a lot of value also to that kind of more subtle approach. Healthy, Wealthy, and Wise has proper foods, good, balanced stuff, and it's fresh. Even more important, it's made with an attitude of devotion, which means a lot. When you know someone has begrudgingly cooked something, it doesn't taste as nice as when someone has done it to try and please God, to offer it to Him first. Just that in itself makes all the food taste so much nicer.

Mukunda: Paul and Linda McCartney have *prasādam* frequently from Healthy, Wealthy, and Wise. Not long ago, Paul met a devotee near his London studio and wrote a song about it. In an interview with James Johnson in a London paper, he said, "One song, 'One of These Days,' is about when I met someone on the way to the studio who was a Hare Kṛṣṇa and we got talking about life-styles and so forth. I'm not a Hare Kṛṣṇa myself, but I'm very sympathetic."

You've been a vegetarian for years, George. Have you had any difficulties maintaining it?

George: No. Actually, I wised up and made sure I had dahl bean soup or something every day. Actually, lentils are one of the cheapest things, but they give you A-1 protein. People are simply screwing up when they go out and buy beef steak, which is killing them with cancer and heart troubles. The stuff costs a fortune too. You could feed a thousand people with lentil soup for the cost of half a dozen filets. Does that make sense?

Mukunda: One of the things that really has a profound effect on people when they visit the temples or read our books is the paintings and sculptures done by our devotee artists of scenes from Kṛṣṇa's pastimes when He appeared on earth five thousand years ago. Prabhupāda once said that these paintings were "windows to the spiritual world," and he organized an art academy, training his disciples in the techniques for creating transcendental art. Now, tens of thousands of people have these paintings hanging in their homes, either the originals, lithographs, canvas prints, or posters. You've been to our multimedia *Bhagavad-gītā* museum in Los Angeles. What kind of an effect did it have on you?

George: I thought it was great—better than Disneyland, really. I mean, it's as valuable as that or the Smithsonian Institute in Washington. The sculpted dioramas look great, and the music is nice. It gives people a real feel for what the kingdom of God must be like, and much more basic than that, it shows in a way that's easy for even a child to understand exactly how the body is different from the soul, and how the soul's the important thing. I always have pictures around like the one of Kṛṣṇa on the chariot that I put in the *Material World* album, and I have the sculpted Siva fountain* the devotees made for me in my garden. Pictures are helpful when I'm chanting. You know that painting in the *Bhagavad-gītā* of the Supersoul in the heart of the dog, the cow, the elephant, the poor man, and the priest? That's very good to help you realize that Kṛṣṇa is dwelling in the hearts of everybody. It doesn't matter what kind of body you've got, the Lord's there with you. We're all the same really.

Meeting Śrīla Prabhupāda

Mukunda: George, you and John Lennon met Śrīla Prabhupāda together when he stayed at John's home, in September of 1969.

George: Yes, but when I met him at first, I underestimated him. I didn't realize it then, but I see now that because of him, the *mantra* has spread so far in the last sixteen years, more than it had in the last five centuries. Now that's pretty amazing, because he was getting older and older, yet he was writing his books all the time. I realized later on that he was much more incredible than what you could see on the surface.

Mukunda: What about him stands out the most in your mind?

George: The thing that always stays is his saying, "I am the servant of the servant of the servant." I like that. A lot

---

* After seeing the dioramas at the Los Angeles *Bhagavad-gītā* museum, George asked if the artists and sculptors who had produced the museum could sculpt a life-sized fountain of Lord Siva, one of the principal Hindu demigods and a great devotee of Lord Kṛṣṇa. Lord Śiva, in a meditative pose, complete with a stream of water spouting from his head, now resides in the gardens of George's estate, heralded as among the most beautiful in all of England.

of people say, "I'm it. I'm the divine incarnation. I'm here, and let me hip you." You know what I mean? But Prabhupāda was never like that. I liked Prabhupāda's humbleness. I always liked his humilty and his simplicity. The servant of the servant of the servant is really what it is, you know. None of us are God—just His servants. He just made me feel so comfortable. I always felt very relaxed with him, and I felt more like a friend. I felt that he was a good friend. Even though he was at the time seventy-nine years old, working practically all through the night, day after day, with very little sleep, he still didn't come through to me as though he was a very highly educated intellectual being, because he had a sort of childlike simplicity. Which is great, fantastic. Even though he was the greatest Sanskrit scholar and a saint, I appreciated the fact that he never made me feel uncomfortable. In fact, he always went out of his way to make me feel comfortable. I always thought of him as sort of a lovely friend, really, and now he's still a lovely friend.

Mukunda: In one of his books, Prabhupāda said that your sincere service was better than some people who had delved more deeply into Kṛṣṇa consciousness but could not maintain that level of commitment. How did you feel about this?

George: Very wonderful, really. I mean it really gave me hope, because as they say, even one moment in the company of a divine person, Kṛṣṇa's pure devotee, can help a tremendous amount.

And I think Prabhupāda was really pleased at the idea that somebody from outside of the temple was helping to get the album made. Just the fact that he was pleased was encouraging to me. I knew he liked "The Hare Krishna Mantra" record, and he asked the devotees to play that song "Govinda." They still play it, don't they?

Mukunda: Every temple has a recording of it, and we play it each morning when the devotees assemble before the altar, before *kīrtana.* It's an ISKCON institution, you might say.

George: And if I didn't get feedback from Prabhupāda on my songs about Kṛṣṇa or the philosophy, I'd get it from the devotees. That's all the encouragement I needed, really. It just seemed that anything spiritual I did, either through songs, or helping with publishing the books, or whatever, really pleased him. The song I wrote, "Living in the Material World," as I wrote in *I, Me, Mine,* was influenced by Śrīla Prabhupāda. He's the one who explained to me how we're not these physical bodies. We just happen to be in them.

Like I said in the song, this place's not really what's happening. We don't belong here, but in the spiritual sky:

As I'm fated for the material world
Get frustrated in the material world
Senses never gratified
Only swelling like a tide
That could drown me in the material world

The whole point to being here, really, is to figure a way to get out.

That was the thing about Prabhupāda, you see. He didn't just talk about loving Kṛṣṇa and getting out of this place, but he was the perfect example. He talked about always chanting, and he was always chanting. I think that that in itself was perhaps the most encouraging thing for me. It was enough to make me try harder, to be just a little bit better. He was a perfect example of everything he preached.

Mukunda: How would you describe Śrīla Prabhupāda's achievements?

George: I think Prabhupāda's accomplishments are very

significant; they're huge. Even compared to someone like William Shakespeare, the amount of literature Prabhupāda produced is truly amazing. It boggles the mind. He sometimes went for days with only a few hours sleep. I mean even a youthful, athletic young person couldn't keep the pace he kept himself at seventy-nine years of age.

Śrīla Prabhupāda has already had an amazing effect on the world. There's no way of measuring it. One day I just realized, "God, this man is amazing!" He would sit up all night translating Sanskrit into English, putting in glossaries to make sure everyone understands it, and yet he never came off as someone above you. He always had that childlike simplicity, and what's most amazing is the fact that he did all this translating in such a relatively short time—just a few years. And without having anything more than his own Kṛṣṇa consciousness, he rounded up all these thousands of devotees, set the whole movement in motion, which became something so strong that it went on even after he left.* And it's still escalating even now at an incredible rate. It will go on and on from the knowledge he gave. It can only grow and grow. The more people wake up spiritually, the more they'll begin to realize the depth of what Prabhupāda was saying–how much he gave.

Mukunda: Did you know that complete sets of Prabhupāda's books are in all the major colleges and universities in the world, including Harvard, Yale, Princeton, Oxford, Cambridge, and the Sorbonne?

George: They should be! One of the greatest things I noticed about Prabhupāda was the way he would be talking to you in English, and then all of a sudden he would say it to you in Sanskrit and then translate it back into English. It was clear that he really knew it well. His

* His Divine Grace A. C. Bhaktivedanta Swami Prabhupāda left this material world on Nov. 14, 1977.

contribution has obviously been enormous from the literary point of view, because he's brought the Supreme Person, Kṛṣṇa, more into focus. A lot of scholars and writers know the *Gītā,* but only on an intellectual level. Even when they write "Kṛṣṇa said . . . ," they don't do it with the *bhakti* or love required. That's the secret, you know—Kṛṣṇa is actually a person who is the Lord and who will also appear there in that book when there is that love, that *bhakti.* You can't understand the first thing about God unless you love Him. These big so-called Vedic scholars—they don't necessarily love Kṛṣṇa, so they can't understand Him and give Him to us. But Prabhupāda was different.

Mukunda: The Vedic literatures predict that after the advent of Lord Caitanya five hundred years ago, there would be a Golden Age of ten thousand years, when the chanting of the holy names of God would completely nullify all the degradations of the modern age, and real spiritual peace would come to this planet.

George: Well, Prabhupāda's definitely affected the world in an absolute way. What he was giving us was the highest literature, the highest knowledge. I mean there just isn't anything higher.

Mukunda: You write in your autobiography that "No matter how good you are, you still need grace to get out of the material world. You can be a *yogī* or a monk or a nun, but without God's grace you still can't make it." And at the end of the song "Living in the Material World," the lyrics say, "Got to get out of this place by the Lord Śrī Kṛṣṇa's grace, my salvation from the material world." If we're dependent on the grace of God, what does the expression "God helps those who help themselves" mean?

George: It's flexible, I think. In one way, I'm never going to get out of here unless it's by His grace, but then again, His grace is relative to the amount of desire I can manifest in myself. The amount of grace I would expect from God should be equal to the amount of grace I can gather or earn. I get out what I put in. Like in the song I wrote about Prabhupāda:

The Lord loves the one that loves the Lord
And the law says if you don't give,
then you don't get loving
Now the Lord helps those that help themselves
And the law says whatever you do
It comes right back on you

—"The Lord Loves the One that Loves the Lord"
from *Living in the Material World*
Apple LP

Have you heard that song "That Which I Have Lost" from my new album, *Somewhere in England*? It's right out of the *Bhagavad-gītā*. In it I talk about fighting the forces of darkness, limitations, falsehood, and mortality.

God Is a Person

Mukunda: Yes, I like it. If people can understand the Lord's message in *Bhagavad-gītā,* they can become truly happy.

A lot of people, when they just get started in spiritual life, worship God as impersonal. What's the difference between worshiping Kṛṣṇa, or God, in His personal form and worshiping His impersonal nature as energy or light?
George: It's like the difference between hanging out with a computer or hanging out with a person. Like I said earlier, "If there is a God, I want to see Him," not only His energy or His light, but Him.
Mukunda: What do you think is the goal of human life?

George: Each individual has to burn out his own *karma* and escape from the chains of *māyā** (illusion), reincarnation, and all that. The best thing anyone can give to humanity is God consciousness. Then you can really give them something. But first you have to concentrate on your own spiritual advancement; so in a sense we have to become selfish to become selfless.
Mukunda: What about trying to solve the problems of life without employing the spiritual process?
George: Life is like a piece of string with a lot of knots tied in it. The knots are the *karma* you're born with from all your past lives, and the object of human life is to try and undo all those knots. That's what chanting and meditation in God consciousness can do. Otherwise you simply tie another ten knots each time you try to undo one knot. That's how *karma* works. I mean, we're now the results of our past actions, and in the future we'll be the results of the actions we're performing now. A little understanding of "As you sow, so shall you reap" is important, because then you can't blame the condition you're in on anyone else. You know that it's by your own actions you're able to get more in a mess or out of one. It's your own actions that relieve or bind you.
Mukunda: In the *Śrīmad-Bhāgavatam,* the crest jewel of all the Vedic literatures, it's described how those pure souls who live in the spiritual world with God have different types of *rasas,*† or relationships, with Him. Is there any special way you like to think of Kṛṣṇa?

---

* The illusory energy that forces the pure soul to think that he is a material body and thus become entangled in material life.

† When a materially conditioned soul becomes completely purified, he returns back home to the spiritual world, where he can enter into a number of intimate relationships with God, based on the degree of his love for Kṛṣṇa. One may relate with the Supreme Lord as servant, friend, parent, or lover. All of

George: I like the idea of seeing Kṛṣṇa as a baby, the way He's often depicted in India. And also Govinda, the cowherd boy. I like the idea that you can have Kṛṣṇa as a baby and feel protective to Him, or as your friend, or as the guru or master-type figure.

"My Sweet Lord"

Mukunda: I don't think it's possible to calculate just how many people were turned on to Kṛṣṇa consciousness by your song "My Sweet Lord." But you went through quite a personal thing before you decided to do that song. In your book you said, "I thought a lot about whether to do 'My Sweet Lord' or not because I would be committing myself publicly . . . Many people fear the words *Lord* and *God* . . . I was sticking my neck out on the chopping block . . . but at the same time I thought 'Nobody's saying it . . . why should I be untrue to myself?' I came to believe in the importance that if you feel something strong enough, then you should say it.

"I wanted to show that *Hallelujah* and *Hare Kṛṣṇa* are quite the same thing. I did the voices singing 'Hallelujah' and then the change to 'Hare Kṛṣṇa' so that people would be chanting the *mahā-mantra*—before they knew what was going on! I had been chanting Hare Kṛṣṇa for a long time, and this song was a simple idea of how to do a Western pop equivalent of a *mantra* which repeats over and over again the holy names. I don't feel guilty or bad about it; in fact it saved many a heroin addict's life."

Why did you feel you wanted to put Hare Kṛṣṇa on the album at all? Wouldn't "Hallelujah" alone have been good enough?

George: Well, first of all "Hallelujah" is a joyous expres-

---

these relationships in the kingdom of God are completely spiritual and are not tinged by the contaminations that affect similar relationships in the material world.

sion the Christians have, but "Hare Kṛṣṇa" has a mystical side to it. It's more than just glorifying God; it's asking to become His servant. And because of the way the *mantra* is put together, with the mystic spiritual energy contained in those syllables, it's much closer to God than the way Christianity currently seems to be representing Him. Although Christ in my mind is an absolute *yogī,* I think many Christian teachers today are misrepresenting Christ. They're supposed to be representing Jesus, but they're not doing it very well. They're letting him down very badly, and that's a big turn off.

My idea in "My Sweet Lord," because it sounded like a "pop song," was to sneak up on them a bit. The point was to have the people not offended by "Hallelujah," and by the time it gets to "Hare Kṛṣṇa," they're already hooked, and their foot's tapping, and they're already singing along "Hallelujah," to kind of lull them into a sense of false security. And then suddenly it turns into "Hare Kṛṣṇa," and they will all be singing that before they know what's happened, and they will think, "Hey, I thought I wasn't supposed to like Hare Kṛṣṇa!"

People write to me even now asking what style that was. Ten years later they're still trying to figure out what the words mean. It was just a little trick really. And it didn't offend. For some reason I never got any offensive feedback from Christians who said "We like it up to a point, but what's all this about Hare Kṛṣṇa?"

Hallelujah may have originally been some mantric thing that got watered down, but I'm not sure what it really means. The Greek word for Christ is *Kristos,* which is, let's face it, Kṛṣṇa, and Kristos is the same name actually.

Mukunda: What would you say is the difference between the Christian view of God, and Kṛṣṇa as represented in the *Bhagavad-gītā?*

George: When I first came to this house, it was occupied by nuns. I brought in this poster of Viṣṇu [a four-armed form of Kṛṣṇa]. You just see His head and shoulders and His four arms holding a conchshell and various other symbols, and it has a big *oṁ** written above it. He has a nice aura around Him. I left it by the fireplace and went out into the garden. When we came back in the house, they all pounced on me, saying, "Who is that? What is it?" as if it were some pagan god. So I said, "Well, if God is unlimited, then He can appear in any form, whichever way He likes to appear. That's one way. He's called Viṣṇu." It sort of freaked them out a bit, but the point is, why should God be limited? Even if you get Him as Kṛṣṇa, He is not limited to that picture of Kṛṣṇa. He can be the baby form, He can be Govinda and manifest in so many other well-known forms. You can see Kṛṣṇa as a little boy, which is how I like to see Kṛṣṇa. It's a joyful relationship. But there's this morbid side to the way many represent Christianity today, where you don't smile, because it's too serious, and you can't expect to see God—that kind of stuff. If there is God, we must see Him, and I don't believe in the idea you find in most churches, where they say, "No, you're not going to see Him. He's way up above you. Just believe what we tell you and shut up."

I mean, the knowledge that's given in Prabhupāda's books—the Vedic stuff—that's the world's oldest scriptures. They say that man can become purified, and with divine vision he can see God. You get pure by chanting, then you see Him. And Sanskrit, the language they're written in, is the world's first recorded language. *Devanāgarī* [the alphabet of the Sanskrit language] actually means "language of the gods."

Mukunda: Anyone who is sincere about making spiritual

---

* This transcendental syllable, which represents Kṛṣṇa, has been chanted by many persons throughout history for spiritual perfection.

advancement, whatever one's religion may be, can usually see the value of chanting. I mean if that person was really trying to be God conscious and trying to chant sincerely.
George: That's right. It's a matter of being open. Anyone who's open can do it. You just have to be open and not prejudiced. You just have to try it. There's no loss, you know. But the "intellectuals" will always have problems, because they always need to "know." They're often the most spiritually bankrupt people, because they never let go; they don't understand the meaning of "to transcend" the intellect. But an ordinary person's more willing to say, "Okay. Let me try it and see if it works." Chanting Hare Kṛṣṇa can make a person a better Christian, too.

Karma and Reincarnation

Mukunda: In *I, Me, Mine,* you speak about *karma* and reincarnation, and how the only way to get out of the cycle is to take up a bona fide spiritual process. You said at one point, "Everybody is worried about dying, but the cause of death is birth, so if you don't want to die, you don't get born!" Did any of the other Beatles believe in reincarnation?
George: I'm sure John does! And I wouldn't want to underestimate Paul and Ringo. I wouldn't be surprised if they're hoping it's true, you know what I mean? For all I know, Ringo might be a *yogī* disguised as a drummer!
Mukunda: Paul has our latest book, *Coming Back: the Science of Reincarnation.* Where do you think John's soul is now?
George: I should hope that he's in a good place. He had the understanding, though, that each soul reincarnates until it becomes completely pure, and that each soul finds its own level, designated by reactions to its actions in this and previous lives.

Mukunda: Bob Dylan did a lot of chanting at one time. He used to come to the Los Angeles temple and came to the Denver and Chicago temples as well. In fact he drove across the United States with two devotees once and wrote several songs about Kṛṣṇa. They spent a lot of time chanting.

George: That's right. He said he enjoyed the chanting and being with them. Also Stevie Wonder had you on one of his records, you know. And it was great the song he put the chanting in—"Pastimes Paradise."

Mukunda: When you were in Vṛndāvana, India, where Lord Kṛṣṇa appeared, and you saw thousands of people chanting Hare Kṛṣṇa, did it strengthen your faith in the idea of chanting to see a whole city living Hare Kṛṣṇa?

George: Yeah, it fortifies you. It definitely helps. It's fantastic to be in a place where the whole town is doing it. And I also had the idea that they were all knocked out at the idea of seeing some white person chanting on beads. Vrndavana is one of the holiest cities in India. Everyone, everywhere, chants Hare Kṛṣṇa. It was my most fantastic experience.

Mukunda: You wrote in your book: "Most of the world is fooling about, especially the people who think they control the world and the community. The presidents, the politicians, the military, etc., are all jerking about, acting as if they are Lord over their own domains. That's basically Problem One on the planet."

George: That's right. Unless you're doing some kind of God conscious thing and you know that He's the one who's really in charge, you're just building up a lot of *karma* and not really helping yourself or anybody else. There's a point in me where it's beyond sad, seeing the state of the world today. It's so screwed up. It's terrible, and it will be getting worse and worse. More concrete everywhere, more pollution, more radioactivity. There's no wilderness left, no pure air. They're chopping the forests down. They're polluting all the oceans. In one sense, I'm pessimistic about the future of the planet. These big guys don't realize for everything they do, there's a reaction. You have to pay. That's *karma.*

Mukunda: Do you think there's any hope?

George: Yes. One by one, everybody's got to escape *māyā.* Everybody has to burn out his *karma* and escape reincarnation and all that. Stop thinking that if Britain or America or Russia or the West or whatever becomes superior, then we'll beat them, and then we'll all have a rest and live happily ever after. That doesn't work. The best thing you can give is God consciousness. Manifest your own divinity first. The truth is there. It's right within us all. Understand what you are. If people would just wake up to what's real, there would be no misery in the world. I guess chanting's a pretty good place to start.

Mukunda: Thanks so much, George.

George: All right. Hare Kṛṣṇa!

The Beatles outside "the Temple" at John Lennon's estate.

2

Chanting for Liberation

A conversation about the Hare Kṛṣṇa *mantra* between Śrīla Prabhupāda and John Lennon, Yoko Ono, and George Harrison

Montreal Star, *June, 1969:*

Reporter: Where do you get your strength?
John Lennon: From Hare Kṛṣṇa.
Yoko: That's where we get it from, you know. We're not denying it.

*In September 1969, A. C. Bhaktivedanta Swami Prabhupāda, founder-*ācārya *(spiritual master) of the Hare Kṛṣṇa movement, arrived as a house guest at Tittenhurst Park, the beautiful eighty-acre British estate owned by John Lennon. Three or four times a week, the Swami, who later became known to the world as Śrīla Prabhupāda, gave public lectures in a tall, stately building at the northern end of the property a hundred yards from the main house, in which John and Yoko lived.*

The building had been formerly used as a hall for chamber-music recitals, but now several of Śrīla Prabhupāda's disciples, who resided along with him in a block of guest houses on the property, installed a small Deity altar and a podium for Śrīla Prabhupāda. The building never really had a name, but after Śrīla Prabhupāda's arrival, everyone called it "the Temple."

They called it "the Temple" for years afterwards, and except for the addition of an enormous crimson-and-gold pipe organ nearly covering the towering west wall, it existed almost unchanged, surrounded by a recording studio complex owned by Ringo Starr.

On September 14, John, Yoko, and George Harrison, after enjoying an Indian vegetarian meal prepared by the devotees at the Temple, walked over to Śrīla Prabhupāda's quarters for their first meeting.

Which Mantra to Chant

Yoko Ono: If Hare Kṛṣṇa is such a strong, powerful *mantra,* is there any reason to chant anything else? For instance, you talked about songs and different *mantras.* Is there any point in the chanting of another song or *mantra*?

Śrīla Prabhupāda: There are other *mantras,* but the Hare Kṛṣṇa *mantra* is especially recommended for this age. But other Vedic *mantras* are also chanted. As I told you, the sages would sit with musical instruments, like the *tamboura,* and chant them. For instance, Nārada Muni* is always chanting *mantras* and playing his stringed instrument, the *vīṇā.* So chanting out loud, with musical instruments, is not a new thing. It's been done since time immemorial. But the chanting of the Hare Kṛṣṇa *mantra* is especially recommended for this age. This is stated in many Vedic literatures, such as the *Brahmāṇḍa Purāṇa,* the *Kali-santaraṇa Upaniṣad,* and the *Agni Purāṇa.* And apart from the statements of the Vedic literature, Lord Kṛṣṇa Himself, in the form of Lord Caitanya, preached that everyone should chant the Hare Kṛṣṇa *mantra.* And many people followed

---

*A liberated sage who travels throughout the universe preaching love of God.

Him. When a scientist discovers something, it becomes public property. People may take advantage of it. Similarly, if a *mantra* has potency, all people should be able to take advantage of it. Why should it remain secret? If a *mantra* is valuable, it is valuable for everybody. Why should it be for only a particular person?

John Lennon: If all *mantras* are just the name of God, then whether it's a secret *mantra* or an open *mantra* it's all the name of God. So it doesn't really make much difference, does it, which one you sing?

Śrīla Prabhupāda: It *does* make a difference. For instance, in a drug shop they sell all types of medicines for curing different diseases. But still you have to get a doctor's prescription in order to get a particular type of medicine. Otherwise, the druggist won't supply you. You might go to the drug shop and say, "I'm diseased. Please give me any medicine you have." But the druggist will ask you, "Where is your prescription?"

Prescription for the Age of Kali

Similarly, in this age of Kali* the Hare Kṛṣṇa *mantra* is prescribed in the *śāstras,* or scriptures. And the great teacher Caitanya Mahāprabhu, whom we consider to be an incarnation of God, also prescribed it. Therefore, our principle is that everyone should follow the prescription of the great authorities. *Mahājano yena gataḥ sa panthāḥ*. We should follow in the footsteps of the great authorities. That is our business. The *Mahābhārata* states, "Dry arguments are inconclusive. A great personality whose opinion does not differ from others' is not considered a

---

*The present age, which began five thousand years ago, characterized in the ancient Vedic scriptures as the age of quarrel and hypocrisy.

great sage. Simply by studying the *Vedas,* which are variegated, one cannot come to the right path by which religious principles are understood. The solid truth of religious principles is hidden in the heart of an unadulterated, self-realized person. Consequently, as the *śāstras* affirm, one should accept whatever progressive path the *mahājanas* advocate." [*Mahābhārata, Vana-parva,* 313.117] This Vedic *mantra* says that if you simply try to argue and approach the Absolute Truth, it is very difficult. By argument and reason it is very difficult, because our arguments and reason are limited. And our senses are imperfect. There are many confusing varieties of scriptures, and every philosopher has a different opinion, and unless a philosopher defeats other philosophers, he cannot become recognized as a big philosopher. One theory replaces another, and therefore philosophical speculation will not help us arrive at the Absolute Truth. The Absolute Truth is very secret. So how can one achieve such a secret thing? You simply follow the great personalities who have already achieved success. So our Kṛṣṇa consciousness philosophical method is to follow the great personalities, such as Lord Kṛṣṇa, Lord Caitanya, and the great spiritual masters in disciplic succession. Take shelter of bona fide authorities and follow them—that is recommended in the *Vedas.* That will take you to the ultimate goal.

You Can't Manufacture a Mantra

Evaṁ paramparā-prāptam: In this way, by disciplic succession, the knowledge is coming down. *Sa kāleneha mahatā yogo naṣṭaḥ parantapa:* But in the course of time the succession was broken. Therefore, Kṛṣṇa says, I am speaking it to you again. So a *mantra* should be received from the disciplic succession. The Vedic injunction is *sampradāya-vihīnā ye mantrās te niṣpalā matāḥ*. If your *mantra* does not come through the disciplic succession, it will not be effective. *Mantrās te niṣphalāḥ. Niṣphalāḥ* means that it will not produce the desired result. So the *mantra* must be received through the proper channel, or it will not act. A *mantra* cannot be manufactured. It must come from the original Supreme Absolute, coming down through the channel of disciplic succession. It has to be received in that way, and only then will it act.

According to our Kṛṣṇa consciousness philosophy, the *mantra* is coming down through four channels of disciplic succession: one through Lord Śiva, one through the goddess Lakṣmī, one through Lord Brahmā, and one through the four Kumāras. The same thing comes down through different channels. These are called the four *sampradāyas,* or disciplic successions. So, one has to take his *mantra* from one of these four *sampradāyas;* then only is that *mantra* active. If we receive the *mantra* in that way, it will be effective. And if one does not receive his *mantra* through one of these *sampradāya* channels, then it will not act; it will not give fruit.

Yoko Ono: If the *mantra* itself has such power, does it matter where you receive it, where you take it?

Śrīla Prabhupāda: Yes, it does matter. For instance, milk is nutritious. That's a fact; everyone knows. But if milk is touched by the lips of a serpent, it is no longer nutritious. It becomes poisonous.

Yoko Ono: Well, milk is material.

Śrīla Prabhupāda: Yes, it is material. But since you are trying to understand spiritual topics through your material senses, we have to give material examples.

Yoko Ono: Well, no, I don't think you have to give me the material sense. I mean, the *mantra* is not material. It should be something spiritual; therefore, I don't think anybody should be able to spoil it. I wonder if anybody can actually spoil something that isn't material.

Śrīla Prabhupāda: But if you don't receive the *mantra* through the proper channel, it may not really be spiritual.

John Lennon: How would you know, anyway? How are you able to tell? I mean, for any of your disciples or us or anybody else who goes to any spiritual master—how are we to tell if he's for real or not?

Śrīla Prabhupāda: You shouldn't go to just *any* spiritual master.

Who's a Genuine Guru?

John Lennon: Yes, we should go to a true master. But how are we to tell one from the other?

Śrīla Prabhupāda: It is not that you can go to just any spiritual master. He must be a member of a recognized *sampradāya,* a particular line of disciplic succession.

John Lennon: But what if one of these masters who's not in the line says exactly the same thing as one who is? What if he says his *mantra* is coming from the *Vedas* and he seems to speak with as much authority as you? He could probably be right. It's confusing—like having too many fruits on a plate.

Śrīla Prabhupāda: If the *mantra* is actually coming through a bona fide disciplic succession, then it will have potency.

John Lennon: But the Hare Kṛṣṇa *mantra* is the best one?

Śrīla Prabhupāda: Yes.

Yoko Ono: Well, if Hare Kṛṣṇa is the best one, why should we bother to say anything else other than Hare Kṛṣṇa?

Śrīla Prabhupāda: It's true, you don't have to bother with anything else. We say that the Hare Kṛṣṇa *mantra* is sufficient for one's perfection, for liberation.

George Harrison: Isn't it like flowers? Somebody may prefer roses, and somebody may like carnations better. Isn't it really a matter for the individual devotee to decide? One person may find that Hare Kṛṣṇa is more beneficial to his spiritual progress, and yet another person may find that some other *mantra* may be more beneficial for himself. Isn't it just a matter of taste, like choosing a flower? They're all flowers, but some people may like one better than another.

Śrīla Prabhupāda: But still there is a distinction. A fragrant rose is considered better than a flower without any scent.

Yoko Ono: In that case, I can't—

Śrīla Prabhupāda: Let's try to understand this flower example.

Yoko Ono: O.K.

Śrīla Prabhupāda: You may be attracted by one flower, and I may be attracted by another flower. But among the flowers a distinction can be made. There are many flowers that have no fragrance and many that have fragrance.

Yoko Ono: Is that flower that has fragrance better?

Śrīla Prabhupāda: Yes. Therefore, your attraction for a particular flower is not the solution to the question of which is actually better. In the same way, personal attraction is not the solution to choosing the best spiritual process. In *Bhagavad-gītā* [4.11], Lord Kṛṣṇa says, "All of them—as they surrender unto Me—I reward accordingly. Everyone follows My path in all respects, O son of Pṛthā." Kṛṣṇa is the Supreme Absolute. If someone wants to enjoy a particular relationship with Him, Kṛṣṇa presents Himself in that way. It's just like the flower example. You may want a yellow flower, and that flower may not have any fragrance. That flower is there; it's for you, that's all. But if someone wants a rose, Kṛṣṇa gives him a rose. You both get the flower of your choice, but when you make a comparative study of which is better, the rose will be considered better.

Yoko Ono: I see a pattern in what you've said. For instance, you said that Hare Kṛṣṇa is the most superpowerful word. And if that is true, then why do we bother to utter any other words? I mean, is it necessary? And why do you encourage us, saying that we're songwriters and all, to write any other song than Hare Kṛṣṇa?

Śrīla Prabhupāda: Chanting the Hare Kṛṣṇa *mantra* is the recommended process for cleaning our hearts. So actually one who chants Hare Kṛṣṇa regularly doesn't have to do anything else. He is already in the correct position. He doesn't have to read any books.

Yoko Ono: Yes, I agree. So why do you say that it's all right to write songs, speak, and all that? It's a waste of time, isn't it?

Śrīla Prabhupāda: No, it's not a waste of time. For instance, Śrī Caitanya Mahāprabhu would spend most of His time simply chanting. He was a *sannyāsī,* a member of the renounced spiritual order of life. So, He was criticized by great *sannyāsīs,* who said, "You have become a *sannyāsī,* and yet You do not read the *Vedānta-sūtra.* You are simply chanting and dancing." In this way, they criticized His constant chanting of Hare Kṛṣṇa. But when Caitanya Mahāprabhu met such stalwart scholars, He did not remain silent. He established the chanting of Hare Kṛṣṇa by sound arguments based on the Vedic scriptures.

Chanting for Liberation

Chanting Hare Kṛṣṇa is sufficient for liberation; there is no doubt about it. But if someone wants to understand the Hare Kṛṣṇa *mantra* through philosophy, through study, through *Vedānta,* then we do not lack information. We have many books. But it is not that the Hare Kṛṣṇa *mantra* is somehow insufficient and therefore we are recommending books. The Hare Kṛṣṇa *mantra* is sufficient. But when Caitanya Mahāprabhu was chanting, He sometimes had to meet opposing scholars, such as Prakāśānanda Sarasvatī and Sārvabhauma Bhaṭṭācārya. And then He was ready to argue with them on the basis of *Vedānta*. So, we should not be dumb. If someone comes to argue with *Vedānta* philosophy, then we must be prepared. When we are preaching, many different types of people will come with questions. We should be able to answer them. Otherwise, the Hare Kṛṣṇa *mantra* is sufficient. It does not require any education, any reading, or anything else. Simply by chanting Hare Kṛṣṇa, you get the highest perfection. That's a fact.

Śrīla Prabhupāda in New York's Tompkins Square Park, Summer 1966. The *East Village Other* said that "he had succeeded in convincing the world's toughest audience that he knew the way to God."

3

Śrīla Prabhupāda Brings the Hare Kṛṣṇa Mantra to the West

When His Divine Grace A. C. Bhaktivedanta Swami Prabhupāda first arrived in America in the midst of the cultural turmoil of the sixties, he quickly captured the hearts and minds of the New York hippies and the San Francisco flower children with the chanting of the Hare Kṛṣṇa mantra.

In 1969 he journeyed to London, and by 1971 Hare Kṛṣṇa had been recorded on hit records by former Beatles John Lennon and George Harrison. By then the mantra *had been heard by hundreds of millions of people, and the International Society for Krishna Consciousness, formed in New York in 1966, had spread to six continents. How could an elderly Indian swami in a strange, foreign land, with no money, no support, no friends, and no followers, achieve such phenomenal success? The story that follows includes eyewitness accounts and excerpts from* Śrīla Prabhupāda-līlāmṛta, *the authorized biography of this extraordinary saint, written by one of his intimate disciples, Satsvarūpa dāsa Goswami.*

The arduous sea voyage from Calcutta to Boston was finally over. The lone passenger aboard the cargo ship *Jaladuta,* a seventy-year-old Indian holy man, had been given free passage by the owner of the Scindia Steamship Company. His Divine Grace A. C. Bhaktivedanta Swami Prabhupāda arrived at Commonwealth Pier on September 17, 1965.

For thousands of years *kṛṣṇa-bhakti,* love of Kṛṣṇa, had been known only in India, but now, on the order of his spiritual master, Śrīla Prabhupāda had come to awaken the natural, dormant Kṛṣṇa consciousness of the American people.

On his arrival day onboard the *Jaladuta,* he wrote in his diary the following words:

> Absorbed in material life, they [Americans] think themselves very happy and satisfied, and therefore they have no taste for the transcendental message of Vāsudeva [Kṛṣṇa]. . . . But I know that Your causeless mercy can make everything possible, because You are the most expert mystic . . . How will I make them understand this message of Kṛṣṇa consciousness? . . . O Lord, I am simply praying for Your mercy so that I will be able to convince them about Your message. . . . I am seeking Your benediction . . . I have no devotion, nor do I have any knowledge, but I have strong faith in the holy name of Kṛṣṇa. . . .

In 1922, Śrīla Prabhupāda's spiritual master, His Divine Grace Bhaktisiddhānta Sarasvatī Ṭhākura, had requested him to spread the teachings of Lord Krsna, including the Hare Kṛṣṇa *mantra,* to the West, and now, after a lifetime in preparation, Śrīla Prabhupāda was ready to begin.

After landing in America with the Indian rupee equivalent of eight dollars, he spent his first year in the United

States with a family in Butler, Pennsylvania; an Indian *yoga* teacher in Manhattan; and later, with the help of friends, rented a small room in upper Manhattan.

By the summer of 1966, he had found a larger location more suited to propagating the Hare Kṛṣṇa *mahā-mantra* and the ancient science of Kṛṣṇa consciousness. That summer Prabhupāda had met a young man named Harvey Cohen, who offered him an old artist-in-residence loft in lower Manhattan's Bowery.

Here, a small group of young Bohemian types would join Śrīla Prabhupāda every Monday, Wednesday, and Friday evening for chanting Hare Kṛṣṇa and classes on the *Bhagavad-gītā*. Although not yet incorporated or known by its present name, the International Society for Krishna Consciousness had been born.

Few of Śrīla Prabhupāda's guests, whose interests included music, drugs, macrobiotics, pacifism, and spiritual meditation, knew very much about what they were chanting or exactly why they were chanting it. They just enjoyed it and liked being in the presence of the man they affectionately called "Swamiji." These musicians, artists, poets, and intellectuals, most of whom had chosen to live outside of mainstream society, felt that by chanting Hare Kṛṣṇa they were taking part in something mystical and unique.

Śrīla Prabhupāda led the solo chanting: Hare Kṛṣṇa, Hare Kṛṣṇa, Kṛṣṇa Kṛṣṇa, Hare Hare/ Hare Rāma, Hare Rāma, Rāma Rāma, Hare Hare. The melody was always the same—a simple four-note phrase, the first four notes of the major scale. Prabhupada led the *kīrtana* with small three-inch-diameter hand cymbals he had brought with him from India. He would ring them in a one-two-*three,* one-two-*three* fashion. Some of his followers clapped along with him, and some joined in with small finger-cymbals of their own. Others sat in *yoga* postures, hands outstretched, chanting and meditating on this novel transcendental vibration. Guests would sometimes bring other instruments, including guitars, tambouras,* flutes, tambourines, and a wide variety of drums.

After a few months some of Śrīla Prabhupāda's followers secured for him a better place to live and spread the chanting of the holy name. The new Second Avenue location on the hippie-filled Lower East Side included an apartment for Śrīla Prabhupāda one floor up and a ground-floor storefront, which he would use as a temple. Within a few weeks, the small sixty-by-twenty-five-foot storefront was packed with young people three nights a week. Gradually the storefront took on the appearance of a temple as visitors began to bring tapestries and paintings for the walls, carpets for the floors, and amplification equipment for Śrīla Prabhupāda's lectures and *kīrtanas* (congregational chanting).

Prabhupāda's *kīrtanas* were lively and captivating, with numerous guests spontaneously rising to their feet, clapping and dancing. Śrīla Prabhupāda, always conducting the *kīrtana* in call-and-response fashion and playing a small African bongolike drum, would accelerate the chant faster and faster, until after about half an hour it would reach a climax and suddenly end. Chanting along with Śrīla Prabhupāda in this small room on Second Avenue, guests found themselves transported into another dimension, a *spiritual* dimension, in which the anxieties and pressures of everyday life in New York City simply did not exist. Many soon caught on that chanting Hare Kṛṣṇa was an intense and effective form of meditation, a direct means of communion with something greater than themselves, no matter what their conception of the Absolute.

Śrīla Prabhupāda initiated his first disciples in Sep-

* An Indian stringed instrument.

tember of '66, at which time about a dozen students vowed to chant a minimum of sixteen rounds a day on their beads. This meant reciting the sixteen-word *mantra* 1,728 times a day, a meditation that would take them between one and a half to two hours to complete.

Prabhupāda's flock soon began to print and distribute invitations and leaflets such as this one:

Practice the transcendental sound vibration,
Hare Krishna, Hare Krishna, Krishna Krishna, Hare Hare
Hare Rama, Hare Rama, Rama Rama, Hare Hare.
This chanting will cleanse the dust from the
mirror of the mind.

Another invited America's youth to

STAY HIGH FOREVER!
No More Coming Down

Practice Krishna Consciousness
Expand your consciousness by practicing the

TRANSCENDENTAL SOUND VIBRATION

HARE KRISHNA, HARE KRISHNA
KRISHNA KRISHNA, HARE HARE
HARE RAMA, HARE RAMA
RAMA RAMA, HARE HARE

In the mornings Śrīla Prabhupāda would lead the devotees in one round of *japa* (chanting on beads). After chanting with Prabhupāda, the devotees would chant their remaining fifteen rounds on their own.

The celebrated American poet Allen Ginsberg, accompanying the *kīrtana* on his harmonium, had by now become a regular at the evening chanting sessions at the temple and in nearby Tompkins Square Park. In a 1980 interview published in Śrīla Prabhupāda's biography, he recalled his experiences.

Allen: *I liked immediately the idea that Swami Bhaktivedanta had chosen the Lower East Side of New York for his practice. . . . I was astounded that he'd come with the chanting, because it seemed like a reinforcement from India. I had been running around singing Hare Kṛṣṇa but had never understood exactly why or what it meant. . . . I thought it was great now that he was here to expound on the Hare Kṛṣṇa* mantra—*that would sort of justify my singing. I knew what I was doing, but I didn't have any theological background to satisfy further inquiry, and here was someone who did. So I thought that was absolutely great. . . . If anyone wanted to know the technical intricacies and the ultimate history, I could send them to him. . . . he had a personal, selfless sweetness like total devotion. And that was what always conquered me . . . a kind of personal charm, coming from dedication . . . I always liked to be with him.*

The chanting of Hare Kṛṣṇa seemed to spread in an almost magical way, and as time went on, the number of people attracted to it increased geometrically. Even in this unlikely New York setting, the *mantra* seemed to have a life of its own. Whether it was the melody, the beat, the sound of the words, the look of the devotees, or Prabhupāda's humility or serenity, nearly everyone who then came in touch with the chanting of Hare Kṛṣṇa responded favorably.

In December 1966, Śrīla Prabhupāda would explain on his first record album, the LP that introduced two of the Beatles, John Lennon and George Harrison, to Hare Kṛṣṇa, that "the chanting Hare Kṛṣṇa, Hare Kṛṣṇa, Kṛṣṇa Kṛṣṇa, Hare Hare/ Hare Rāma, Hare Rāma, Rāma Rāma, Hare Hare is not a material sound vibration, but comes directly from the spiritual world."

Prabhupāda's Tompkins Square Park *kīrtanas* were spiritual happenings that are now legendary. Hundreds of people from all walks of life took part; some as observers and some as eager participants, chanting, clapping their hands, dancing, and playing musical instruments. Irving Halpern, one of many local musicians who regularly participated, remembers the scene.

Irving: *The park resounded. The musicians were very careful in listening to the* mantras. . . . *I have talked to a couple of musicians about it, and we agreed that in his head this Swami must have had hundreds and hundreds of melodies that had been brought back from the real learning from the other side of the world. So many people came there just to tune in to the musical gift, the transmission of the* dharma. *"Hey," they would say, "listen to this holy monk." People were really sure there were going to be unusual feats, grandstanding, flashy levitations, or whatever people* expected *was going to happen. But when the simplicity of what the Swami was really saying, when you began to sense it—whether you were motivated to actually make a lifetime commitment and go this way of life, or whether you merely wanted to place it in a place and give certain due respect to it—it turned you around.*

And that was interesting, too, the different ways in which people regarded the kīrtana. *Some people thought it was a prelude. Some people thought it was a main event. Some people liked the music. Some people liked the poetic sound of it.*

After the *kīrtanas* Śrīla Prabhupāda usually spoke for a few minutes about Kṛṣṇa consciousness, inviting everyone back to the temple for a Sunday afternoon "love festival" of chanting and feasting, a weekly event that soon became a tradition that continues today. The October 9 edition of the *New York Times* described the

Tompkins Square Park *kīrtana* with the following headline: "SWAMI'S FLOCK CHANTS IN PARK TO FIND ECSTASY."

> Sitting under a tree in a Lower East Side park and occasionally dancing, fifty followers of a Hindu swami repeated a sixteen-word chant for two hours yesterday afternoon to the accompaniment of cymbals, tambourines, sticks, drums, bells, and a small reed organ. . . . Repetition of the chant, Swami A. C. Bhaktivedanta says, is the best way to achieve self-realization in this age of destruction.
>
> . . . many in the crowd of about a hundred persons standing around the chanters found themselves swaying to or clapping hands in time to the hypnotic rythmic music. "It brings a state of ecstasy," said Allen Ginsberg the poet. " . . . The ecstasy of the chant or mantra Hare Krishna, Hare Krishna, Krishna Krishna, Hare Hare/ Hare Rama, Hare Rama, Rama Rama, Hare Hare has replaced LSD and other drugs for many of the Swami's followers."

At the same time, New York's avant-garde newspaper *The East Village Other* ran a front page story with a full-page photograph of Śrīla Prabhupāda standing and speaking to a large group of people in the park. The banner headline read "SAVE EARTH NOW!!" and in large type just below the picture, the *mahā-mantra* was printed: "HARE KRISHNA HARE KRISHNA KRISHNA KRISHNA HARE HARE HARE RAMA HARE RAMA RAMA RAMA HARE HARE." The article admired the chanting and described how Śrīla Prabhupāda "had succeeded in convincing the world's toughest audience—Bohemians, acidheads, potheads, and hippies—that he knew the way to God."

> Turn Off, Sing Out, and Fall In. This new brand of holy man, with all due deference to Dr. Leary, has come forth

> with a brand of "Consciousness Expansion" that's sweeter than acid, cheaper than pot, and nonbustible by fuzz.

The newspaper story described how a visit to the temple at 26 Second Avenue would bring "living, visible, tangible proof" that God is alive and well. The story quoted one of Śrīla Prabhupāda's new disciples:

> I started chanting to myself, like the Swami said, when I was walking down the street—Hare Krishna, Hare Krishna, Krishna Krishna, Hare Hare/ Hare Rama, Hare Rama, Rama Rama, Hare Hare—over and over, and suddenly everything started looking so beautiful, the kids, the old men and women . . . even the creeps looked beautiful. . . to say nothing of the trees and flowers.

Finding it superior to the euphoria from any kind of drug, he said,

> There's no coming down from this. I can always do this any time, anywhere. It is always with you.

To San Francisco and Beyond

Early in 1967, several of Śrīla Prabhupāda's disciples left New York and opened a temple in the heart of San Francisco's Haight-Ashbury district, home for thousands of hippies and "flower children" from all over the country. Within a short time, Śrīla Prabhupāda's temple there had become a spiritual haven for troubled, searching, and sometimes desperate young people. Drug overdoses were common, and hundreds of confused, dazed, and disenchanted young Americans roamed the streets.

Haridāsa, the first president of the San Francisco temple, remembers what it was like.

Haridāsa: *The hippies needed all the help they could get, and they knew it. And the Rādhā-Kṛṣṇa temple was certainly a kind of spiritual haven. Kids sensed it. They were running, living on the streets, no place where they could go, where they could rest, where people weren't going to hurt them.*

I think it saved a lot of lives; there might have been a lot more casualties if it hadn't been for Hare Kṛṣṇa. It was like opening a temple in a battlefield. It was the hardest place to do it, but it was the place where it was most needed. Although the Swami had no precedents for dealing with any of this, he applied the chanting with miraculous results. The chanting was wonderful. It worked.

Michael Bowen, an artist and one of the leading figures of the Haight-Ashbury scene, recalled that Śrīla Prabhupāda had "an amazing ability to get people off drugs, especially speed, heroin, burnt-out LSD cases—all of that."

Every day at the temple devotees cooked and served to over two hundred young people a free, sumptuous multicourse lunch of vegetarian food offered to Kṛṣṇa. Many local merchants helped to make this possible by donating to the cause. An early San Francisco devotee recalls those days.

Harṣarāṇī: *People who were plain lost or needed comforting . . . sort of wandered or staggered into the temple. Some of them stayed and became devotees, and some just took* prasādam [*spiritual food*] *and left. Just from a medical standpoint, doctors didn't know what to do with people on LSD. The police and the free clinics in the area couldn't handle the overload of people taking LSD. The police saw Swamiji* [*Śrīla Prabhupāda*] *as a certain refuge.*

Throughout lunch, devotees played the New York recording of Śrīla Prabhupāda chanting the Hare Kṛṣṇa *mantra*. The sacred sound reinforced the spiritual mood of the temple and helped to ease the tensions and frustrations of its young guests.

Sunday, January 29, 1967 marked the major spiritual event of the San Francisco hippy era, and Śrīla Prabhupāda, who was ready to go anywhere to spread Kṛṣṇa consciousness, was there. The Grateful Dead, Moby Grape, Janis Joplin and Big Brother and the Holding Company, Jefferson Airplane, Quicksilver Messenger Service—all the new-wave San Francisco bands—had agreed to appear with Śrīla Prabhupāda at the Avalon Ballroom's Mantra-Rock Dance, proceeds from which would go to the local Hare Kṛṣṇa temple.

Thousands of hippies, anticipating an exciting evening, packed the hall. LSD pioneer Timothy Leary dutifully paid the standard $2.50 admission fee and entered the ballroom, followed by Augustus Owsley Stanley II, known for his own brand of LSD.

At about 10:00 P.M., Śrīla Prabhupāda and a small entourage of devotees arrived amid uproarious applause and cheering by a crowd that had waited weeks in great anticipation for this moment. Śrīla Prabhupāda was given a seat of honor onstage and was introduced by Allen Ginsberg, who explained his own realizations about the Hare Kṛṣṇa *mahā-mantra* and how it had spread from the small storefront in New York to San Francisco. The well-known poet told the crowd that the chanting of the Hare Kṛṣṇa *mantra* in the early morning at the Rādhā-Kṛṣṇa temple was an important community service to those who were "coming down from LSD," because the chanting would "stabilize their consciousness on reentry."

The chanting started slowly but rythmically, and little by little it spread throughout the ballroom, enveloping everyone. Hippies got to their feet, held hands, and began to dance as enormous, pulsing pictures of Kṛṣṇa were projected around the walls of the ballroom in perfect sync with the beat of the *mantra.* By the time Śrīla Prabhupāda stood and began to dance with his arms raised, the crowd was completely absorbed in chanting, dancing, and playing small musical instruments they had brought for the occasion.

Ginsberg later recalled, "We sang Hare Kṛṣṇa all evening. It was absolutely great—an open thing. It was the height of the Haight-Ashbury spiritual enthusiasm."

As the tempo speeded up, the chanting and dancing became more and more intense, spurred on by a stageful of top rock musicians, who were as charmed by the magic of the *mahā-mantra* as the amateur musicians had been at the Tompkins Square *kīrtanas* only a few weeks before. The chant rose; it seemed to surge and swell without limit. When it seemed it could go no further, the chanting stopped. Śrīla Prabhupāda offered prayers to his spiritual master into the microphone and ended by saying three times, "All glories to the assembled devotees!" The Haight-Ashbury neighborhood buzzed with talk of the Mantra-Rock Dance for weeks afterward.

Within a few months of the Mantra-Rock event, devotees in San Francisco, New York, and Montreal began to take to the streets with their *mṛdaṅgas* (clay drums) and *karatālas* (hand cymbals) to chant the *mahā-mantra* on a daily basis. In just a few years, temples were opening all over North America and Europe, and people everywhere were hearing the chanting of Hare Kṛṣṇa.

On May 31, 1969, when the Vietnam war protest movement was reaching its climax, six devotees joined John Lennon and Yoko Ono in their Montreal hotel room to play instruments and sing on John and Yoko's famous recording "Give Peace a Chance." This song, which included the *mantra,* and a hit single, "The Hare Krishna

Mantra," produced in September of the same year by Beatle George Harrison and featuring the devotees, introduced millions to the chanting. Even Broadway's long-running musical hit *Hair* included exuberant choruses of the Hare Kṛṣṇa *mantra.*

At the now historic mass antiwar demonstration in Washington, D.C., on November 15, 1969, devotees from all over the United States and Canada chanted the Hare Kṛṣṇa *mantra* throughout the day and distributed "The Peace Formula," a small leaflet based on Śrīla Prabhupāda's teachings from the Vedic scriptures. "The Peace Formula," which proposed a spiritual solution to the problem of war, was distributed en masse for many months and influenced thousands of lives.

By 1970, when George Harrison's "My Sweet Lord"—with its beautiful recurring lyrics of Hare Kṛṣṇa and Hare Rāma—was the international number-one hit song of the day, devotees in *dhotis* and *sārīs,* chanting the *mahā-mantra* with musical instruments, were now a familiar sight in almost every major city throughout the world. Because of Śrīla Prabhupāda's deep love for Lord Kṛṣṇa and his own spiritual master, his amazing determination, and his sincere compassion, "Hare Kṛṣṇa" had become a household word.

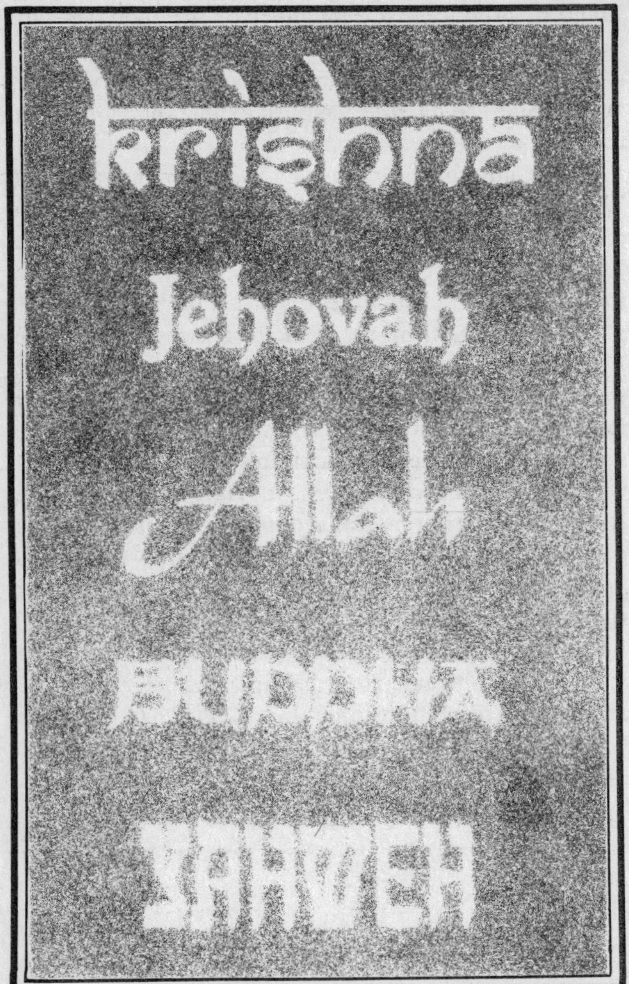

"All God's names are hallowed."—Theologian Martin Buber
The above names for God are considered sacred by five of the world's major religions.

His Divine Grace A. C. Bhaktivedanta Swami Prabhupada, founder-*acarya* (spiritual master) of the International Society for Krishna Consciousness, who brought the Hare Krsna *mantra* to the West, chants on beads.

Photo: Jerry Kozinski

George Harrison practices *mantra* meditation by chanting Hare Krsna on beads, above, and joins devotees from the London temple for *kirtana* (group meditation), below.

George Harrison and Patti Boyd with Srila Prabhupada and a disciple at George's home in England, 1969.

Śrīla Prabhupāda leads the chanting of Hare Kṛṣṇa at Golden Gate Park, San Francisco, during the historic "summer of love," 1967. (p. 57; artist: Locana dāsa)

This poster advertised San Francisco's major spiritual happening of the 1960s—The Mantra-Rock Dance at the Avalon Ballroom, featuring Śrīla Prabhupāda, Allen Ginsberg, and the most popular new rock bands of the day. (p. 59)

Śrī Caitanya, center, an incarnation of Lord Kṛṣṇa, leads His followers in the chanting of Hare Kṛṣṇa. Lord Caitanya taught that the chanting of

God's holy names is the universal spiritual practice for the modern age.
(p. 78; artist: Parīkṣit dāsa)

In one of the most astounding religious conversions of all time, Prakāśānanda Sarasvatī surrendered to Lord Caitanya. (p. 81; artist: Muralīdhara dāsa)

4

Chanting for Higher Consciousness: A Cultural History

It's a scene that has been repeated countless times on the thoroughfares of cities throughout the Western world—from Hollywood Boulevard and Fifth Avenue in America, to London's Oxford Street and the Champs Élysées in Paris. There, in the midst of traffic, shops, restaurants, and movie theaters, people suddenly find themselves confronted by a group of young persons singing and dancing to the beat of cylindrical drums and the brassy cadence of hand cymbals. The men are dressed in flowing robes and have shaven heads; the women wear colorful Indian *sārīs*. Of course, it's the Hare Kṛṣṇa people, chanting their now familiar *mantra*, Hare Kṛṣṇa, Hare Kṛṣṇa . . . But what's actually going on? Is it some form of protest, avant-garde street theater, a religious demonstration, or what?

If you were to ask them, you'd learn that these people are performing a type of meditation long encouraged and practiced in the West—the chanting of the holy names of God. (*Kṛṣṇa* is the Sanskrit name for the Supreme Lord.) Of course, meditation is a word that's thrown around quite loosely these days. It's come to mean practically any technique employed to silence and calm the harried modern mind. But the ancient and authorized form of meditation practiced by Hare Kṛṣṇa people has a much deeper and more sublime purpose. Although it easily soothes the turbulent mind, it also awakens those who chant it to their original, joyful spiritual nature and consciousness, imparting a genuine sense of pleasure unavailable by any other means.

The *Vedas,* scriptures containing the timeless spiritual knowledge of ancient India, state that such an awakening process is desperately needed because everyone in this material world is in a sleeping, dreamlike condition. We have forgotten our original, spiritual identity, accepting instead a temporary material body composed of physical elements as our real self. The *Vedas* compare the material body to the subtle forms we experience in dreams. While sleeping, we forget our normal waking identity and may find ourselves enjoying or suffering in different types of bodies. But when we hear the ringing of the alarm clock, we awaken and return to normal consciousness. We remember who we are and what we should be doing. Similarly, by hearing the powerful transcendental sound vibrations of the Hare Kṛṣṇa *mantra,* we can gradually wake up to our original self, the soul, which is characterized by eternality and is full of knowledge and ever-increasing pleasure.

The sages of ancient India therefore tell us that the goal of human life should not be to try to enjoy our temporary dreamlike situation in the material world. Rather, we are advised to awaken to our original, spiritual nature and ultimately return to our true home in the spiritual world, where we may enjoy an eternal relationship with the Supreme Personality of Godhead, Lord Kṛṣṇa.

This search for the true self through the meditative process is not something recently discovered , nor is it in any way alien to the basically rationalistic philosophical and spiritual traditions of the West. Although Western civilization has for the most part directed its energies outward in various efforts to control and exploit the resources of nature, there have always been inner-directed philosophers, saints, and mystics who have dedicated themselves to a higher purpose than material well-being, which is in all cases temporary.

The Search for the Self

The Greek philosophers Socrates and Plato held a view of man's original nature quite similar to that of the Vedic sages. This temporary world, they taught, is not our real home; we once existed in a *spiritual* world. In Plato's famous dialogues, Socrates says that in our original condition, "We were pure ourselves and not yet enshrined in that living tomb which we carry about, now that we are imprisoned in the body like an oyster in his shell."[1] The purpose of philosophy, for these early Athenian thinkers, was to awaken a person to his original, spiritual identity, now hidden within the covering of the physical body.

The very same thing was taught in Galilee four hundred years later by Jesus Christ. In the Gospel of St. John, Christ says, "It is the spirit that quickeneth [gives life], the flesh profiteth nothing."[2] In other words, the body is simply an external covering for the soul, which is the real life-giving force. Therefore, Jesus warned, "What profiteth a man if he gain the whole world, but lose his immortal soul?"[3] The highest goal of life, Christ taught, is to understand and experience our inner spiritual nature. In the Gospel of St. Luke, Jesus instructs mankind to look within for true spiritual life: "Neither shall they say, Lo here! or lo there! for behold, the kingdom of God is within you."[4]

Describing his inner search for God through meditation, St. Augustine, a great saint and eminent philosopher of the Roman Catholic Church, tells us in his *Confessions* how his mind "withdrew its thoughts from experience, abstracting itself from the contradictory throng of sensuous images."[5]

During the Middle Ages in Europe, there was widespread interest in meditation, with many saints and philosophers writing of their thoughts about the inward quest for divine reality. Thomas à Kempis, in his classic *Imitation of Christ,* cautions man about material life and summarizes the purpose and goal of meditation: "What do you seek here, since this world is not your resting place? Your true home is in Heaven; therefore remember that all things of this world are transitory. All things are passing and yourself with them. See that you do not cling to them, lest you become entangled and perish with them. Let all your thoughts be with the Most High."[6]

When one achieves this deep spiritual vision, his entire world view is competely transformed, as in the case of St. Francis of Assisi, who devoted his life to prayer and meditation. In his *Life of St. Francis,* St. Bonaventura says, "In all fair things, he beheld Him who is most fair, and, through the traces of Him which He has implanted in all His creatures, he was led on to reach the All-loved, constructing of these things a ladder whereby he might ascend to Him who is Loveliness itself . . ."[7] In other words, when one's original, spiritual consciousness is revived, one sees God everywhere and in everything. One enters a unique world of spiritual knowledge and pleasure, far superior to what most of us perceive as reality—a spiritual reality that lies just beyond our ordinary abilities of perception. William James, the American philosopher who specialized in the psychology of religion, writing on this point, said, "Our normal waking consciousness, rational consciousness as we call it, is but one special type of consciousness, whilst all about it, parted from it by the filmiest of screens, there lie potential forms of consciousness entirely different. We may go throughout life without suspecting their existence, but apply the requisite stimulus, and at a touch they are there in all their completeness. . . ."[8]

But what is the "requisite stimulus" for awakening the dormant consciousness of the self and God that lies within everyone's heart? All genuine spiritual authorities agree that such transcendental experiences cannot be awakened by any material stimulus or experience, including ingestion of chemical substances like LSD and other "mind-expanding" drugs.

When Śrīla Prabhupāda, the founder-*acarya* (spiritual master) of the Hare Kṛṣṇa movement, was asked by a follower of Timothy Leary about LSD's place in man's spiritual life, he said that drugs were not necessary for spiritual life, that they could not produce spiritual consciousness, and that all drug-induced "religious visions" were simply hallucinations. To realize God was not so easy or cheap that one could do it just by taking a pill or smoking.[9]

Sound and Self-Realization

The Vedic scriptures advise that the proper technique for awakening spiritual consciousness is the hearing and chanting of transcendental sounds or *mantras,* like the Hare Kṛṣṇa *mantra.* The power of sound to effect changes in consciousness has long been recognized. The English philosopher and statesman Sir Francis Bacon noted that "the sense of hearing striketh the spirit more immediately than any other senses."[10]

Ordinary *material* sounds, however, will not awaken

spiritual consciousness. For this, one must hear *spiritual* sound vibrations. Therefore, almost every religion in the world recommends that we meditate upon the Word of God. St. John wrote in his Gospel, "In the beginning was the Word, and the Word was with God, and the Word was God."[11] Divine sound is thus of a vastly different quality than worldly or material sound. This fact was clearly explained by St. Augustine in his *Confessions.* Once, as he emerged from a mystic trance, he said he "heard again the babble of our own tongues, wherein each word has a beginning and an ending. Far unlike Thy Word, our Lord, who abideth in Himself, never growing old and making all things new."[12] And in the Gospel of St. John, Christ says, "The words that I speak unto you, they are spirit."[13]

While the Word, or teachings of God, have enormous power to transform and uplift our lives, just as important are the actual names of God, which are sometimes praised aloud in song or quietly meditated upon. Since God is fully spiritual and absolute, the Vedic scriptures inform us that His holy names are invested with the Lord's full spiritual potencies. God and His name are the same. The *Padma Purāṇa* states, "There is no difference between the holy name of the Lord and the Lord Himself. As such, the holy name is as perfect as the Lord Himself." The Stoic philosopher Maximus noted, "There is one supreme God who is, as it were, the God and mighty father of all." "It is Him," he said, "whom we worship under many names."[14] Modern Jewish theologian Martin Buber also agreed that "All God's names are hallowed."[15]

And the Bible is replete with similar statements. In the Old Testament it is said, "The name of the Lord is a strong tower: the righteous runneth into it and is safe."[16] In Psalms, King David proclaims, "I will praise the name of God with a song."[17] Indeed, the Psalms contain countless references to the name of God: "All nations whom Thou hast made shall come and worship before Thee, O Lord:

and shall glorify Thy name.[18] . . . O give thanks unto the Lord: call upon His name: make known His deeds among the people. Sing unto Him, sing psalms unto Him: talk ye of all His wondrous works. Glory ye in His holy name.[19] . . . Praise Him with the timbrel and dance: praise Him with stringed instruments and organs. Praise Him upon the loud cymbals."[20] The prophet Isaiah described God as "One that inhabiteth eternity, and whose name is Holy."[21] Centuries later, Israel Baal Shem Tov (1699-1761), the great Jewish mystic, founded Hasidism, a popular pietist movement within Judaism, in which members dance and chant in glorification of the Supreme Lord.

Christ, when teaching his disciples how to pray, glorified the Lord's holy name: "Our Father, who art in Heaven, hallowed be Thy name." And in his Epistle to the Romans, St. Paul wrote, "For whosoever shall call upon the name of the Lord shall be saved."[22]

In the early Christian churches, there was, according to the historian Eusebius, "one common consent in chanting forth the praises of God."[23] The Gregorian chants, popularized in the sixth century by Pope Gregory the Great and later by works like Handel's masterpiece the *Messiah,* with its resounding choruses of *hallelujah* ("praised be the Lord"), are still performed and appreciated all over the world.

In addition to praising the Lord's name and glories in song, there also developed in the Christian churches the practice of meditating upon God by chanting prayers on rosary beads, a tradition continued today by millions of Catholics worldwide. John Chrysostom, a saint of the Greek Orthodox church, especially recommended the "prayerful invocation of the name of God," which he said should be practiced "uninterrupted."[24] The repetition of the Jesus prayer ("Lord Jesus, Son of God, have mercy on me") became a regular practice among members of the Eastern Church. In *The Way of a Pilgrim,* a Russian monk describes this form of meditation: "The continuous interior prayer of Jesus is a constant uninterrupted calling upon the divine name of Jesus with the lips, in the spirit, in the heart. . . . One who accustoms himself to this appeal experiences as a result so deep a consolation and so great a need to offer the prayer always, that he can no longer live without it."[25]

Among the followers of Islam, the names of God (Allah) are held sacred and meditated upon. According to tradition, there are ninety-nine names of Allah, called "the Beautiful Names." They are found inscribed on monuments such as the Taj Mahal and on the walls of mosques. These names are chanted on an Islamic rosary, which consists of three sets of thirty-three beads. Worshipers repeat the names to help them concentrate their minds upon Allah. The dual titles Al-Rahman, al-Rahim, meaning "God, the compassionate, the merciful," are invoked at the beginning of each chapter of the Koran. Other Arabic names of God glorify Him as the creator, provider, and king.

In India, the Sikhs place special emphasis on the name of God. Indeed, the Sikhs call God *Nāma*—"the name." Guru Nanak, the founder of the Sikh religion, prayed, "In the ambrosial hours of the morn I meditate on the grace of the true name," and says that he was instructed by the Lord in a vision to "Go and repeat My name, and cause others to do likewise."[26]

"Rosaries are widely used in Buddhism; large ones by monks, smaller ones by the laity," says Geoffrey Parrinder, a professor of comparative religion at the University of London, in his book *Worship in the World's Religions*. "The large ones have 108 beads, the two halves representing the fifty-four stages of becoming a *boddhisattva* (enlightened one). The large bead in the middle stands for Buddha."

Members of Japan's largest Buddhist order, the Pure

Land sect, practice repetition of the name of Buddha *(namu amida butsu).* The founder Shinran Shonin says, "The virtue of the Holy Name, the gift of him that is enlightened, is spread throughout the world."[27] The Buddhist teachings reveal that by chanting the name of Buddha, the worshiper becomes liberated from the cycle of reincarnation and joins the Buddha in the Pure Land, or spiritual world.

Kṛṣṇa: The All-Encompassing Name of God

Although God is known throughout the world by many different names, each of which describes some particular aspect of His glories and attractive features, there is one name which expresses the sum total of God's infinite qualities and characteristics. This supreme, all-encompassing, and most powerful name of God is found in the oldest religious scriptures in the world, the Sanskrit *Vedas* of India, which state that the principal name of God is Kṛṣṇa.

Śrīla Prabhupāda explains: "When we speak of Kṛṣṇa, we refer to God. There are many names for God throughout the world and throughout the universe, but Kṛṣṇa is the supreme name according to Vedic knowledge."[28] He further states, "God has many names according to His activities, but because He possesses so many opulences, and because with these opulences He attracts everyone, He is called Kṛṣṇa ['all-attractive']."[29]

The spiritual qualities of Kṛṣṇa's holy name are described throughout the Vedic literatures. The *Padma Purāṇa* states, "The holy name of Kṛṣṇa is transcendentally blissful. It bestows all spiritual benedictions, for it is Kṛṣṇa Himself, the reservoir of all pleasure. . . . It is not a material name under any condition, and it is no less powerful than Kṛṣṇa Himself. Since Kṛṣṇa's name is not contaminated by the material qualities, there is no question of its being involved with *māyā* [illusion]. Kṛṣṇa's name is always liberated and spiritual; it is never conditioned by the laws of material nature. This is because the name of Kṛṣṇa and Kṛṣṇa Himself are identical."

Since time immemorial, millions of devotees and saintly persons have chanted the name of Kṛṣṇa to achieve spiritual perfection. But history records that it was widely popularized by Lord Caitanya, an incarnation of Lord Kṛṣṇa who appeared in Bengal barely five centuries ago and established the chanting of the Hare Kṛṣṇa *mantra* as the universal spiritual practice for the present age.

According to Vedic cosmology, the material creation eternally passes through cycles of four ages. Each begins with a Golden Age (Satya-yuga), then conditions progressively deteriorate, ending in the Kali-yuga, an age characterized by quarrel and hypocrisy. For each of the four ages, the *Vedas* prescribe a universal method of self-realization just suited for that particular age.

For instance, in the Satya-yuga, the recommended path was that of the mystic *yoga* system, which involved a lifetime of unbroken yoga practice, accompanied by strict vows of penance and austerity. We are presently at the beginning of the last age, Kali-yuga. In this age people no longer have the endurance, willpower, or sufficient life span necessary to successfully practice the original *yoga* system described in the *Vedas.* The Vedic scriptures therefore advise, "In this age of Kali there is no alternative, there is no alternative, there is no alternative for spiritual progress other than chanting the holy name, chanting the holy name, chanting the holy name of the Lord."[30]

The *Kali-santaraṇa Upaniṣad* specifically recommends the chanting of the Hare Kṛṣṇa *mantra:* "Hare Kṛṣṇa, Hare Kṛṣṇa, Kṛṣṇa Kṛṣṇa, Hare Hare/ Hare Rāma, Hare Rāma, Rāma Rāma, Hare Hare—these sixteen names composed of thirty-two syllables are the only means to counteract the evil effects of Kali-yuga. In all the *Vedas* it is seen that to cross the ocean of nescience there is no alternative to chanting the holy name."

Lord Caitanya's biographers record that He spent many years traveling all over India spreading the chanting of the holy names of Kṛṣṇa. He chanted the Hare Kṛṣṇa *mantra* congregationally (*kīrtana*) to the accompaniment of musical instruments, including drums and hand cymbals. The Lord also chanted the *mantra* quietly a specific number of times daily as a private meditation (*japa*). In the *Śikṣāṣṭaka,* His famous prayers about the holy names of Kṛṣṇa, Lord Caitanya wrote, "Let there be all victory for the chanting of the holy name of Lord Kṛṣṇa, which can cleanse the mirror of the heart and stop the miseries of the blazing fire of material existence. That chanting is the waxing moon that spreads the white lotus of good fortune for all living entities. It is the life and soul of all education. The chanting of the holy name of Kṛṣṇa expands the blissful ocean of transcendental life. It gives a cooling effect to everyone and enables one to taste full nectar at every step."

During His lifetime, Lord Caitanya predicted that the holy names of Kṛṣṇa would spread to every town and village in the world. This prophecy lay unfulfilled for four hundred years, until the time of Bhaktivinoda Ṭhākura, a great spiritual master in the direct line of disciplic succession from Lord Caitanya. In 1885 Bhaktivinoda wrote, "Lord Caitanya did not advent Himself to liberate only a few men in India. Rather, His main objective was to emancipate all living entities of all countries throughout the entire universe and preach the Eternal Religion. . . . There is no doubt that this unquestionable order will come to pass. . . . Very soon the unparalleled path of *hari-nama sankirtana* [the congregational chanting of the holy name of the Lord] will be propagated all over the world. . . . Oh, for that day when the fortunate English,

French, Russian, German, and American people will take up banners, *mridangas* [drums], and *karatalas* [hand cymbals] and raise *kirtana* [chanting] through their streets and towns! When will that day come?"[31]

Bhaktivinoda's vision became a reality in less than a century. In 1965, India's greatest spiritual and cultural ambassador, His Divine Grace A. C. Bhaktivedanta Swami Prabhupāda, arrived in New York's East Village, the heart of the countercultural movement of the sixties. Within a year Śrīla Prabhupāda, tenth in the line of spiritual masters from Lord Caitanya, had founded the International Society for Krishna Consciousness. Very quickly, the sound of the chanting of Hare Kṛṣṇa spread, first across America, then on to England and throughout the world.

The Vedic scriptures predict that although the age of Kali is the most degraded of all, the chanting of the Hare Kṛṣṇa *mantra* will dramatically alter the present war-torn, hate-filled atmosphere of the world. These most ancient, timeless writings forecast a Golden Age, beginning with the widespread chanting of Hare Kṛṣṇa, during which the painful disturbances of this age will be mitigated and people everywhere will be economically, politically, socially, culturally, and spiritually happy.

Śrīla Prabhupāda explains, "Kali-yuga continues for 432,000 years, of which only 5,000 years have passed. Thus there is still a balance of 427,000 years to come. Of these 427,000 years, the 10,000 years of the *saṅkīrtana* movement inaugurated by Śrī Caitanya Mahāprabhu 500 years ago provide the opportunity for the fallen souls of Kali-yuga to take to the Kṛṣṇa consciousness movement, chant the Hare Kṛṣṇa *mahā-mantra,* and thus be delivered from the clutches of material existence and return home, back to Godhead."[32]

NOTES

1. *Phaedrus*, translator Benjamin Jowett.
2. John, 6:63.
3. Mark, 8:36.
4. Luke, 17:21.
5. *Confessions*, translator C. Bigge. London: Methuen and Company, Ltd., p. 244.
6. *Imitation of Christ*, translator Leo Sherley-Price. Baltimore: Penguin Classics edition.
7. *The Life of St. Francis*. New York: Everyman's Library, 1912.
8. *The Varieties of Religious Experience*, William James. London: Longman, Green, and Co., p. 388.
9. *Śrīla Prabhupāda-līlāmṛta*, Satsvarūpa dāsa Goswami. Los Angeles: Bhaktivedanta Book Trust, 1980, p. 201.
10. *Sylva sylvarum*, in *Works*, ed. James Spedding, et. al. New York: 1864, IV, p. 231.
11. John, 1:1.
12. *Confessions*, X, p. 321.
13. John, 6:63.
14. *Comparative Religion*, Esther Carpenter, 1913, p. 35.
15. *Worship in the World's Religions*, Geoffrey Parrinder. London: Faber and Faber, 1961, p. 7.
16. Proverbs, 18:10.
17. Psalms, 69:30.
18. Psalms, 86:9.
19. Psalms, 105:1–4.
20. Psalms, 150:4–5.
21. Isaiah, 57:15.
22. Romans, 10:13.
23. *Ecclesiastical History*.
24. *The Way of a Pilgrim*, translator R.M. French. London: Society for Promoting Christian Knowledge.
25. Ibid.
26. *Japji* (The Meditations of Guru Nanak).
27. *Buddhist Psalms*, Yamabe, S., and Beck, L.A. Murray, 1921, p. 86.
28. *Śrī Nāmāmṛta: The Nectar of the Holy Name*, Los Angeles: Bhaktivedanta Book Trust, 1982, p. 142.
29. Ibid.
30. *Bṛhan-nāradīya Purāṇa*.
31. *Sajjana-toṣaṇī* (newspaper).
32. *Śrī Nāmāmṛta*, p. 249.

After organizing India's largest peaceful civil disobedience movement, Lord Caitanya convinced the Muslim ruler of Navadvīpa to allow the chanting of Hare Kṛṣṇa to be continued unhindered.

5

The Life of Śrī Caitanya

In the latter part of the fifteenth century, India's most extraordinary political, cultural, and religious reformer appeared in a small town in West Bengal.

Five hundred years before Gandhi, this remarkable personality inaugurated a massive nonviolent civil disobedience movement. He swept aside the stifling restrictions of the hereditary caste system and made it possible for people from any station in life to achieve the highest platform of spiritual enlightenment. In doing so, He broke the stranglehold of a proud intellectual elite on India's religious life. Ignoring all kinds of outmoded rituals and formulas, He introduced a revolutionary spiritual movement that was rapidly accepted all over India, a movement which, because of its universal appeal, has now spread all over the world. The name of this powerful reformer was Śrī Kṛṣṇa Caitanya Mahāprabhu, the founder of the modern-day Hare Kṛṣṇa movement.

The Vedic scriptures of India had long predicted His birth, in 1486 in Māyāpur, a quarter of the city of Navadvīpa. Great saints and scholars soon detected that He was not an ordinary human being, but an incarnation of the Supreme Personality of Godhead, Lord Kṛṣṇa Himself, appearing as a great devotee of the Lord.

Caitanya had little patience with ritualistic religious functions, and as He grew to young manhood, He began to carry out His divine mission. He wanted all people, everywhere, to have access to the actual experience of love of God, by which one can feel the highest spiritual ecstasies. This awakening, Śrī Caitanya taught, could be attained by *saṅkīrtana*—the chanting of the holy names of the Lord, the Hare Kṛṣṇa *mantra.*

Caitanya rapidly acquired many followers, who immediately took up the chanting, sometimes performing it in their homes and sometimes in the streets of Navadvīpa. The Lord's *saṅkīrtana* movement immediately threatened the established groups in the social hierarchy—the Muslim rulers of Bengal and the hereditary Hindu priestly class, the caste priests who were attempting to artificially monopolize religious leadership. Members of both groups lodged complaints with the local Muslim ruler, Chand Kazi.

Agreeing that Caitanya and His followers threatened the established order, the Kazi tried to suppress the growing *saṅkīrtana* movement. On his order, constables raided the home of one of Caitanya's followers and smashed the drums used in the chanting. The Kazi ordered that the chanting of the holy names of the Lord be immediately stopped and threatened that if it began again in Navadvīpa, he would ruthlessly punish those responsible.

When informed of the raid, Śri Caitanya immediately organized the largest peaceful civil disobedience movement in Indian history up to that time. On a prearranged evening, Śrī Caitanya and one hundred thousand of His followers suddenly appeared in the streets of Navadvīpa and divided into many well-organized chanting parties. As they danced through the city, the sound of the Hare Kṛṣṇa *mantra* resounded in a deafening roar. Finally, the chanters converged on the residence of the Kazi, who hid inside.

At the Lord's invitation, however, the Kazi appeared, and the two began negotiations. Speaking politely, and with great logic and reason, the Lord convinced the Kazi that the complaints against *saṅkīrtana* were groundless. In a dramatic conversion, the Kazi himself became a follower of Caitanya and actively promoted and protected the *saṅkīrtana* movement. To this very day, Hindus visit the tomb of this Muslim magistrate to pay their respects. Since the time of the Kazi, the Muslim inhabitants of Navadvīpa have never interfered with the public chanting of the Hare Kṛṣṇa *mantra,* even during the time of the Hindu-Muslim riots.

Not long after this important victory in His native town, Śrī Caitanya began to spread His movement all over India. For six years He traveled the length and breadth of the country, chanting the Hare Kṛṣṇa *mantra* and spreading love of God. At many places, crowds of hundreds of thousands of people would join with Him in massive chanting parties. Nevertheless, He also encountered opponents, the strongest of whom were the Māyāvādīs, an elitist group of philosophers who had spread throughout India, twisting the meaning of the Vedic scriptures in a vain attempt to prove that God has no personality or form. The impersonalists also believed that spiritual enlightenment could be obtained only by a chosen few who knew Sanskrit and arduously studied the *Vedānta-sūtra.*

Throughout His travels, Śrī Caitanya struggled against the Māyāvādīs and succeeded in convincing many of them by the strength of His preaching. One of the greatest philosophers of the Māyāvāda school, Sārvabhauma Bhaṭṭācārya, tried to prevail over Śrī Caitanya in philosophical discussion but was defeated. Countering the Bhaṭṭācārya's impersonal explanation of God, Śrī Caitanya said, "The living entities are all individual persons, and they are all parts and parcels of the Supreme Whole.

If the parts and parcels are individual persons, the source of their emanation must not be impersonal. He is the Supreme Person amongst all relative persons." Then out of His causeless mercy, Lord Caitanya performed a wondrous miracle, manifesting before Sārvabhauma Bhaṭṭācārya His beautiful, original, spiritual form as Kṛṣṇa, the Supreme Personality of Godhead. Falling at Lord Caitanya's feet, the former impersonalist philosopher surrendered to Him and soon became a great devotee of the Lord.

But the biggest confrontation with the Māyāvādīs was yet to come, and it occured at their very headquarters, for centuries the capital of the Māyāvāda school, the city of Benares. There Lord Caitanya stayed with His friends and devotees and continued His *saṅkīrtana* movement, attracting crowds of thousands wherever He went. Hearing reports of this, Prakāśānanda Sarasvatī, the leader of the prevailing Māyāvāda sect, began to criticize the Lord. A real spiritual leader, he said, would never involve himself in singing and dancing with all kinds of ordinary people. Ignorant of the spiritual significance of chanting the Hare Kṛṣṇa *mantra,* he considered it mere sentiment. Prakāśānanda Sarasvatī believed a spiritualist should continually study abstract philosophy and engage in lengthy discussions about the Absolute Truth. A great clash between a popular nonsectarian universal religious movement and a stifling, schismatic and separatist philosophy was about to occur. Śrī Caitanya Mahāprabhu would soon destroy forever the impersonalists' attempted domination over Indian spiritual thought and practice.

The Lord's followers were extremely unhappy about the Māyāvādīs' constant criticism of Him, so in order to pacify them, He accepted an invitation to a meeting of all the leading Māyāvādīs. After seating Himself on the ground at the assembly, the Lord, exhibiting His supreme mystic potency, manifested from His body a spiritual effulgence more brilliant than the sun. The Māyāvādīs were amazed and immediately stood in respect. Then Prakāśānanda Sarasvatī inquired about why Caitanya chanted and danced instead of studying *Vedānta* philosophy. Lord Caitanya, who in truth was extremely well versed in the Vedic teachings, replied, "I have taken to the *saṅkīrtana* movement instead of the study of *Vedānta* because I am a great fool." Indirectly, the Lord was criticizing the Māyāvādīs for being overly proud of their dry, intellectual study of the *Vedas,* which had led them to false conclusions. "And because I am a great fool," Caitanya continued, "my spiritual master forbade Me to play with *Vedānta* philosophy. He said that it is better that I chant the holy name of the Lord, for this would deliver Me from bondage." Śrī Caitanya then spoke a Sanskrit verse His spiritual master had told Him to always remember:

harer nāma harer nāma harer nāmaiva kevalam
kalau nāsty eva nāsty eva nāsty eva gatir anyathā

"In this age of Kali, there is no alternative, there is no alternative, there is no alternative for spiritual progress other than the chanting of the holy name, the chanting of the holy name, the chanting of the holy name of the Lord." (*Bṛhan-nāradīya Purāṇa*)

The discussion went on for hours. Finally, in one of the most astounding religious conversions of all time, Prakāśānanda Sarasvatī, the Māyāvādīs' greatest scholar, along with all his followers, surrendered to Lord Caitanya and began to chant the holy names of Kṛṣṇa with great enthusiasm. As a result of this conversion, the entire city of Benares adopted Śrī Caitanya's *saṅkīrtana* movement.

Although born a *brāhmaṇa,* a member of the highest caste, Lord Caitanya always said that such designations were simply external, and He behaved accordingly. Disregarding the social conventions of the age, He would stay in the homes of devotees from even the lowest caste and take His meals with them. Indeed, He delivered His most esoteric teachings on the subject of love of God to Rāmānanda Rāya, a member of a lower caste. Another of the Lord's disciples, Haridāsa Ṭhākura, was born a Muslim and thus was considered an outcast in Hindu society. Yet Śrī Caitanya elevated him to the exalted position of *nāmācārya,* the spiritual master of the holy name of Kṛṣṇa. Śrī Caitanya judged people not by their social status but by their spiritual advancement.

In this way, Lord Caitanya laid the foundation for a universal religion for all mankind, a scientific process of spiritual awakening that is now rapidly spreading around the globe. In this present age, when attendance at churches, temples, and mosques is diminishing daily, and the world is torn with violence between numerous religious and political sects, it is easy to see that people are growing more and more dissatisfied with external, divisive religious formulas.

People are hungering for an experience of spirituality that transcends all boundaries. Millions are now finding that experience in the worldwide *saṅkīrtana* movement of Lord Caitanya, who said, "This *saṅkīrtana* movement is the prime benediction for humanity at large because it spreads the rays of the benediction moon. It is the life of all transcendental knowledge. It increases the ocean of transcendental bliss, and it enables us to fully taste the nectar for which we are always anxious."

The prostitute said, "My dear Haridāsa, O great preacher, great devotee, you are so beautifully built, and your youth is just beginning. Who is the woman who could control her mind after seeing you?"

6

Haridāsa Ṭhākura and the Prostitute

Strict followers of the caste system in sixteenth-century India avoided all contact with Muslims. Yet Śrī Caitanya Mahāprabhu, founder of the modern-day Hare Kṛṣṇa movement, shattered all bonds of prejudice and bigotry by elevating Haridāsa Ṭhākura, who was born in a Muslim family, to the position of nāmācārya, *or the spiritual master of the holy name of Kṛṣṇa. In this way Śrī Caitanya practically demonstrated one of His central teachings—if any person is seen to be a great devotee of the Lord, he should be honored and respected regardless of his birth or social status. Such a spiritually advanced person can completely transform the lives of others. In the following incident from the life of Haridāsa Ṭhākura, we see how a beautiful prostitute, through the power of his chanting, became a great saint.*

In the forest of Benāpola, in what is now known as Bangladesh, the solitary monk sat before the sacred *tulasī* plant chanting the holy names of Kṛṣṇa day and night. Haridāsa Ṭhākura would chant three hundred thousand names of the Lord each day. The body of this extraordinary saint, who was constantly in trance, was maintained by spiritual strength from chanting, and he barely slept at all. He was so influential that all the neighboring people offered their respects to him.

But a landholder named Rāmacandra Khān, the district tax collector, was envious of devotees of Lord Kṛṣṇa. Unable to tolerate the great respect that was being offered to Haridāsa Ṭhākura, he schemed to dishonor him. By no means, however, could he find any fault in the character of Haridāsa. Therefore, he called for some local prostitutes and plotted to discredit the saint. Rāmacandra Khān said to the prostitutes, "There is a mendicant named Haridāsa Ṭhākura. All of you devise a way to deviate him from his vows of austerity." Austerity means renunciation of sensual pleasures, especially the pleasure of sex.

Rāmacandra Khān selected a ravishing young beauty to break the monk's vow of celibacy and dishonor him. "I shall attract the mind of Haridāsa Ṭhākura," she promised, "within three days."

Rāmacandra Khān said to the prostitute, "My constable will go with you so that as soon as he sees you with Haridāsa Ṭhākura, he will immediately arrest him and bring both of you to me."

The prostitute replied, "First let me have union with him once; then the second time I shall take your constable with me to arrest him."

At night the prostitute, after dressing herself in a seductive way, went to the cottage of Haridāsa Ṭhākura. Haridāsa was young, strong, and handsome, and the girl was eager to be alone with him. After offering respects to the *tulasī* plant, she went to the door of Haridāsa's hut, offered him obeisances, and stood there. Exposing part of her body to his view, she sat down on the threshold and spoke to him in sweet words.

"My dear Haridāsa, O great preacher, great devotee, you are so beautifully built, and your youth is just beginning. Who is the woman who could control her mind after seeing you? I am eager to be united with you. My mind is greedy for this. If I don't obtain you, I shall not be able to keep my body and soul together."

Haridāsa Ṭhākura replied, "I shall accept you without fail, but you will have to wait until I have finished chanting my regular rounds on my beads. Until that time, please sit and listen to the chanting of the holy name. As soon as I am finished, I shall fulfill your desire."

Hearing this, the prostitute remained sitting there while Haridāsa Ṭhākura chanted on his beads until the light of morning appeared. When she saw that it was morning, the prostitute stood up and left. Coming before Rāmacandra Khān, she informed him of all the news.

"Today Haridāsa Ṭhākura has promised to enjoy with me," she said. "Tomorrow certainly I shall have union with him."

The next night, when the prostitute came again, Haridāsa Ṭhākura gave her many assurances. "Last night you were disappointed. Please excuse my offense. I shall certainly accept you. Please sit down and hear the chanting of the Hare Kṛṣṇa *mahā-mantra* until my regular chanting is finished. Then your desire will surely be fulfilled."

After offering her obeisances to the *tulasī* plant and Haridāsa Ṭhākura, she again sat down at the door. Hearing Haridāsa Ṭhākura chanting the Hare Kṛṣṇa *mantra,* she also chanted, "O my Lord Hari, O my Lord Hari."

When the night came to an end, the prostitute was restless. Seeing this, Haridāsa said, "I have vowed to chant ten million names in one month. I have taken this vow, but now it is nearing its end. I thought that today I would be able to finish my chanting of the Hare Kṛṣṇa *mantra.* I tried my best to chant the holy name all night, but I still did not finish. Tomorrow I will surely finish, and my vow will be fulfilled. Then it will be possible for me to enjoy with you in full freedom."

The prostitute returned to Rāmacandra Khān and informed him of what had happened. The next day she came earlier, at the beginning of the evening, and stayed all night. Again, as she began to hear Haridāsa Ṭhākura's chanting, she also chanted "Hari, Hari," the holy name of the Lord.

"Today it will be possible for me to finish my chanting," the saint said. "Then I shall satisfy all your desires."

The night ended with Haridāsa still chanting, but now, because of her constant hearing of Haridāsa's chanting, the mind of the prostitute had changed. Now fully purified, she began to cry and fell at the lotus feet of Haridāsa Ṭhākura, confessing that Rāmacandra Khān had appointed her to pollute him.

"Because I have taken the profession of a prostitute," she said, "I have performed unlimited sinful acts. My lord, be merciful to me. Deliver my fallen soul."

Haridāsa replied, "I know everything about the conspiracy of Rāmacandra Khān. He is nothing but an ignorant fool. Therefore his activities do not make me feel unhappy. On the very day Rāmacandra Khān was planning his intrigue against me, I would have left this place immediately, but because you came, I stayed here for three days to deliver you."

"Kindly act as my spiritual master," she begged. "Instruct me in my duty by which to get relief from material existence."

Haridāsa answered, "Immediately go home and distribute to the *brāhmaṇas* [priests] whatever property you have. Then come back to this room and stay here forever in Kṛṣṇa consciousness. Chant the Hare Kṛṣṇa *mantra* continuously and render service to the *tulasī* plant by watering her and offering prayers to her. In this way you will very soon get the opportunity to be sheltered at the lotus feet of Kṛṣṇa."

After thus instructing the prostitute in the chanting of Hare Kṛṣṇa, Haridāsa Ṭhākura stood up and left, continuously chanting the Lord's holy names.

Following the order of her spiritual master, the prostitute distributed to the local priests whatever household possessions she had. Following Haridāsa's example, she began chanting the Hare Kṛṣṇa *mahā-mantra* three hundred thousand times a day. She chanted throughout the entire day and night, and she worshiped the *tulasī* plant. By eating frugally and fasting, she conquered her senses. As soon as her senses were controlled, symptoms of love of God appeared in her person.

Thus the prostitute became a great saint, and her fame spread throughout the land. Because she was very advanced in spiritual life, many devotees of the Lord would come to see her. Seeing the sublime character of this former prostitute, everyone was astonished. They glorified the influence of Haridāsa Ṭhākura and offered their obeisances to him.

As for Rāmacandra Khān, he was eventually ruined by the arrangement of the Lord. Meanwhile, Haridāsa Ṭhākura continued his travels, always preaching the glories of the holy name, about which he often said, "As the rising sun immediately dissipates all the world's darkness, which is deep like an ocean, so the holy name of the Lord, if chanted once without offenses, can dissipate all the reactions of a living being's sinful life. All glories to that holy name of the Lord, which is auspicious for the entire world."

To this day, thousands of pilgrims each year visit the *samadhi* tomb of Haridāsa Ṭhākura, who, although born a Muslim, became the spiritual master of the holy names and one of India's greatest devotee-saints.

"Hare Kṛṣṇa can be chanted by any man in any social position, in any country, and in any age, for Kṛṣṇa is the Supreme Lord of all people, in all social positions, in all countries, in all ages."

7

The Science of *Mantra* Meditation

(Excerpts from the writings of
His Divine Grace
A. C. Bhaktivedanta Swami Prabhupāda)

Reviving Our Original Brilliance

Sparks are beautiful as long as they are in the fire. Similarly, we have to remain in the association of the Supreme Personality of Godhead and always engage in devotional service, for then we shall always be brilliant and illuminating. As soon as we fall from the service of the Lord, our brilliance and illumination will immediately be extinguished, or at least stopped for some time. When we living entities, who are like sparks of the original fire, the Supreme Lord, fall into a material condition, we must take the *mantra* from the Supreme Personality of Godhead as it is offered by Śrī Caitanya Mahāprabhu. By chanting this Hare Kṛṣṇa *mantra,* we shall be delivered from all the difficulties of this material world.

Śrīmad-Bhāgavatam (8.6.15)

The Mantra for Everyone

Caitanya Mahāprabhu introduced the chanting of Hare Kṛṣṇa, Hare Kṛṣṇa, Kṛṣṇa Kṛṣṇa, Hare Hare/ Hare Rāma, Hare Rāma, Rāma Rāma, Hare Hare as a great means of propaganda for spreading love of God. It is not that it is recommended only for Kali-yuga. Actually, it is recommended for every age. There have always been many devotees who have chanted and reached perfection in all ages. That is the beauty of this Kṛṣṇa consciousness movement. It is not simply for one age, or for one country, or for one class of people. Hare Kṛṣṇa can be chanted by any man in any social position, in any country and in any age, for Kṛṣṇa is the Supreme Lord of all people in all social positions, in all countries, in all ages.

Elevation to Kṛṣṇa Consciousness (p. 91)

Awakening Our Original Consciousness

It is said in the *Caitanya-caritāmṛta,* "Pure love for Kṛṣṇa is eternally established in the hearts of living entities. It is not something to be gained from another source. When the heart is purified by hearing and chanting, the living entity naturally awakens." Since Kṛṣṇa consciousness is inherent in every living entity, everyone should be given a chance to hear about Kṛṣṇa. Simply by hearing and chanting—*śravaṇaṁ kīrtanam*—one's heart is directly purified, and one's original Kṛṣṇa consciousness is immediately awakened. Kṛṣṇa consciousness is not artificially imposed upon the heart, it is already there. When one chants the holy name of the Supreme Personality of Godhead, the heart is cleansed of all material contamination.

The Nectar of Instruction, Text 4 (p. 41)

Chanting: The Universal Religion

In this present age quarrels take place even over trifles, and therefore the *śāstras* [scriptures] have recommended for this age a common platform for realization, namely chanting the holy names of the Lord. People can hold meetings to glorify the Lord in their respective languages and with melodious songs, and if such performances are executed in an offenseless manner, it is certain that the participants will gradually attain spiritual perfection without having to undergo more rigorous methods. . . . all people of the world will accept the holy name of the Lord as the common platform for the universal religion of mankind.

Śrīmad-Bhāgavatam (1.1, Intro.)

Seeing God Through Sound

Hare Kṛṣṇa, Hare Kṛṣṇa, Kṛṣṇa Kṛṣṇa, Hare Hare, Hare Rāma, Hare Rāma, Rāma Rāma, Hare Hare is a sound (*śabda*) that is nondifferent from Kṛṣṇa. The sound Kṛṣṇa and the original Kṛṣṇa are the same. . . .

There are things which we hear but do not see—the wind may be whistling past our ears, and we can hear it, but there is no possibility of seeing the wind. Since hearing is no less an important experience or valid one than seeing, we can hear Kṛṣṇa and realize His presence through sound. Śrī Kṛṣṇa Himself says, "I am not there in My abode, or in the heart of the meditating *yogī*, but where My pure devotees are singing." We can feel the presence of Kṛṣṇa as we actually make progress.

Rāja-vidyā: The King of Knowledge (pp. 16–17)

The Holy Name Acts Like Fire

Fire will act, regardless of whether handled by an innocent child or by someone well aware of its power. For example, if a field of straw or dry grass is set afire, either by an elderly man who knows the power of fire or by a child who does not, the grass will be burned to ashes. Similarly, one may or may not know the power of chanting the Hare Kṛṣṇa *mantra,* but if one chants the holy name he will become free from all sinful reactions.

Śrīmad-Bhāgavatam (6.2.18)

Liberation from Ego

The effect of chanting the holy name of the Lord is perceived by the chanter as liberation from the conception of false egoism. False egoism is exhibited by thinking oneself to be the enjoyer of the world and thinking everything in the world to be meant for the enjoyment of one's self only. The whole materialistic world is moving under such false egoism of "I" and "mine," but the factual effect of chanting the holy name is to become free from such misconceptions.

Śrīmad-Bhāgavatam (2.1.11)

Chanting Defeats Death

By the grace of the Lord, if a devotee, at the time of death, can simply chant His holy names—Hare Kṛṣṇa, Hare Kṛṣṇa, Kṛṣṇa Kṛṣṇa, Hare Hare/ Hare Rāma, Hare Rāma, Rāma Rāma, Hare Hare—simply by chanting this *mahā-mantra,* he immediately surpasses the great ocean of the material sky and enters the spiritual sky. He never has to come back for repetition of birth and death. Simply by chanting the holy name of the Lord, one can surpass the ocean of death.

Śrīmad-Bhāgavatam (4.10.30)

Experiencing Ecstasy

The transcendental ecstatic attachment for Kṛṣṇa which results from perfectly understanding that Krsna's person and name are identical is called *bhāva* [ecstatic spiritual emotion]. One who has attained *bhāva* is certainly not contaminated by material nature. He actually enjoys transcendental pleasure from *bhāva*, and when *bhāva* is intensified, it is called love of Godhead. Lord Caitanya taught that the holy name of Kṛṣṇa, called the *mahā-mantra* (great chanting), enables anyone who chants it to attain the stage of love of Godhead, or intensified *bhāva*.

Teachings of Lord Caitanya (p. 207)

The Sound Incarnation of God

Sometimes Krsna descends personally, and sometimes He descends as sound vibration, and sometimes He descends as a devotee. There are many different categories of *avatāras* [incarnations]. In this present age Krsna has descended in His holy name, Hare Kṛṣṇa, Hare Kṛṣṇa, Kṛṣṇa Kṛṣṇa, Hare Hare/ Hare Rāma, Hare Rāma, Rāma Rāma, Hare Hare. Lord Caitanya Mahaprabhu also confirmed that in this age of Kali, Kṛṣṇa has descended in the form of sound vibration. Sound is one of the forms which the Lord takes. Therefore it is stated that there is no difference between Kṛṣṇa and His name.

Elevation to Kṛṣṇa Consciusness (p. 90)

Christ or Kṛṣṇa—the Name's the Same
(from a conversation with a Benedictine monk)

Christos is the Greek version of the word *Kṛṣṇa.* When an Indian person calls on Kṛṣṇa, he often says, "Kṛṣṭa." *Kṛṣṭa* is a Sanskrit word meaning "attraction." So when we address God as "Christ," "Kṛṣṭa," or "Kṛṣṇa," we indicate the same all-attractive Supreme Personality of Godhead. When Jesus said, "Our Father, who art in heaven, sanctified be Thy name," that name of God was "Kṛṣṭa" or "Kṛṣṇa." Actually it doesn't matter—Kṛṣṇa or Christ—the name is the same. The main point is to follow the injunctions of the Vedic scriptures that recommend chanting the name of God in this age. I have not come to teach you, but only to request you to please chant the name of God. The Bible also demands this of you. So let us kindly cooperate and chant, and if you have a prejudice against chanting the name Kṛṣṇa, then chant "Christos" or "Kṛṣṭa"—there is no difference. Śrī Caitanya said: *nāmnām akāri bahudhā nija-sarva-śaktiḥ.* "God has millions and millions of names, and because there is no difference between God's name and Himself, each one of these names has the same potency as God." Therefore, even if you accept designations like "Hindu," "Christian," or "Muhammadan," if you simply chant the name of God found in your own scriptures, you will attain the spiritual platform. We always have these beads, just as you have your rosary. You are chanting, but why don't the other Christians also chant? If you would like to cooperate with us, then go to the churches and chant, "Christ," "Kṛṣṭa," or "Kṛṣṇa." What could be the objection?

Science of Self-Realization (pp. 112–18)

The Wild Horses of the Mind

The mind is always concocting objects for happiness. I am always thinking, "This will make me happy," or "That will make me happy. Happiness is here. Happiness is there." In this way the mind is taking us anywhere and everywhere. It is as though we are riding on a chariot behind an unbridled horse. We have no power over where we are going but can only sit in horror and watch helplessly. As soon as the mind is engaged in the Krsna consciousness process—specifically chanting Hare Kṛṣṇa, Hare Kṛṣṇa, Kṛṣṇa Kṛṣṇa, Hare Hare/ Hare Rāma, Hare Rāma, Rāma Rāma, Hare Hare—then the wild horses of the mind will gradually come under our control.

On the Way to Kṛṣṇa (pp. 13–14)

The Peace Formula

The earth is the property of God, but we, the living entities, especially the so-called civilized human beings, are claiming God's property as our own, under both an individual and collective false conception. If you want peace, you have to remove this false conception from your mind and from the world. This false claim of proprietorship by the human race on earth is partly or wholly the cause of all disturbances of peace on earth.

Foolish and so-called civilized men are claiming proprietary rights on the property of God because they have now become godless. You cannot be happy and peaceful in a godless society. In the *Bhagavad-gītā* Lord Kṛṣṇa says that He is the factual enjoyer of all activities of the living entities, that He is the Supreme Lord of all universes, and that He is the well-wishing friend of all beings. When the people of the world know this as the formula for peace, it is then and there that peace will prevail.

Therefore, if you want peace at all, you will have to change your consciousness into Kṛṣṇa consciousness, both individually and collectively, by the simple process of chanting the holy name of God. This is a standard and recognized process for achieving peace in the world. We therefore recommend that everyone become Kṛṣṇa conscious by chanting Hare Kṛṣṇa, Hare Kṛṣṇa, Kṛṣṇa Kṛṣṇa, Hare Hare/ Hare Rāma, Hare Rāma, Rāma Rāma, Hare Hare.

This is practical, simple, and sublime. Four hundred and eighty years ago this formula was introduced in India by Lord Śrī Caitanya, and now it is available in your country. Take to this simple process of chanting as above mentioned, realize your factual position by reading the *Bhagavad-gītā As It Is,* and reestablish your lost relationship with Kṛṣṇa, God. Peace and prosperity will be the immediate worldwide result.

Science of Self-Realization (pp. 192–93)

Free vs. High-priced Mantras

Recently, an Indian *yogī* came to America to give some "private *mantra.*" But if a *mantra* has any power, why should it be private? If a *mantra* is powerful, why should it not be publicly declared so that everyone can take advantage of it? We are saying that this Hare Kṛṣṇa *mahā-mantra* can save everyone, and we are therefore distributing it publicly, free of charge. . . . The devotees are preaching without charge, declaring in the streets, parks, and everywhere, "Here! Here is the Hare Kṛṣṇa *mahā-mantra.* Come on, take it!"

Path of Perfection (p. 72)

Rx for Heart Disease

(from a conversation with a community relations officer with the Chicago police department)

Lieutenant Mozee: Would there be more of a beneficial influence—more of a strengthening of the community—if the program [congregational chanting] were held in a poorer area rather than an affluent area?

Śrīla Prabhupāda: Our treatment is for the spiritually diseased person. When a person is afflicted with a disease, there are no distinctions between a poor man and a rich man. They are both admitted to the same hospital. Just as the hospital should be in a place where both the poor man and the rich man can easily come, the location of the *saṅkīrtana* facility should be easily accessible to all. Since everyone is materially infected, everyone should be able to take advantage.

So our chanting process is for everyone, because it cleanses the heart, regardless of the man's opulence or poverty. The only way to permanently change the criminal habit is to change the heart of the criminal. As you well know, many thieves are arrested numerous times and put into jail. Although they know that if they commit theft they will go to jail, still they are forced to steal, because of their unclean hearts. Therefore without cleansing the heart of the criminal, you cannot stop crime simply by more stringent law enforcement. The thief and the murderer already know the law, yet they still commit violent crimes, due to their unclean hearts. So our process is to cleanse the heart. Then all the troubles of this material world will be solved.

Science of Self-Realization (p. 170)

Attaining real self-awareness also gives one the ability to see the spiritual nature of all living beings. When our natural, spiritual feelings are awakened, we experience the ultimate unity of all life.

8

The Benefits of Chanting

Dr. Daniel Goleman, associate editor of Psychology Today *and author of* The Varieties of Meditative Experiences, *after studying the meditational techniques of members of the Kṛṣṇa consciousness movement, said, "I found the Hare Kṛṣṇa devotees to be well-integrated, friendly, and productive human beings. In a culture like ours, in which inner, spiritual development is almost totally neglected in favor of materialistic pursuits, we might have something to learn from their meditational practices."*

Everyone knows that a happy life requires good health. Proper diet, adequate exercise, and sufficient rest are necessary to keep our bodies strong and fit. If we neglect these demands, our bodies become weakened and resistance wanes. Highly susceptible to infection, we eventually become ill.

More important, but less well known, is the inner self's need for spiritual nourishment and attention. If we ignore our spiritual health requirements, we become overwhelmed by negative material tendencies like anxiety, hatred, loneliness, prejudice, greed, boredom, envy, and anger.

In order to counteract and prevent these subtle infections of the self, we should, as recommended in the Vedic literatures, incorporate into our lives a program of self-examination and steady inner growth, based on spiritual strength and clarity of thought.

The transcendental potency necessary for developing complete psychological and spiritual fulfillment is already present within everyone. It must, however, be uncovered by a genuine spiritual process. Of all such authentic processes, India's timeless *Vedas* tell us that meditation on the Hare Kṛṣṇa *mantra* is the most powerful.

The initial result of chanting the Hare Kṛṣṇa *mantra* is summarized by Śrīla Prabhupāda in his commentary on the *Bhagavad-gītā:* "We have practical experience that any person who is chanting the holy names of Kṛṣṇa (Hare Kṛṣṇa, Hare Kṛṣṇa, Kṛṣṇa Kṛṣṇa, Hare Hare/ Hare Rāma, Hare Rāma, Rāma Rāma, Hare Hare) in course of time feels some transcendental pleasure and very quickly becomes purified of all material contamination."

In the preliminary stages of chanting, the practitioner experiences a clearing of consciousness, peace of mind, and relief from unwanted drives and habits. As one develops more realization by chanting, he perceives the original, spiritual existence of the self. According to the *Bhagavad-gītā,* this enlightened state "is characterized by one's ability to see the self by the pure mind and to relish and rejoice in the self."

And in the *Caitanya-caritāmṛta,* a seventeen-volume commentary on the life and teachings of Śrī Caitanya, founder of the modern-day Kṛṣṇa consciousness movement, the ultimate benefit of chanting is described. "The result of chanting is that one awakens his love for Kṛṣṇa and tastes transcendental bliss. Ultimately, one attains the association of Kṛṣṇa and engages in His devotional service, as if immersing himself in a great ocean of love."

So by chanting Hare Kṛṣṇa, one reaps innumerable benefits, culminating in Kṛṣṇa consciousness and love of God. We can realize the fruits of chanting by adopting the process of *mantra* meditation and applying it systematically. For clear understanding of the progressive effects of chanting, some of the more important benefits are discussed separately.

Peace of Mind

Initially meditation focuses on controlling the mind, for in our normal condition, we are slaves to any whimsical thoughts, desires, and appetites the mind may generate. We think of something and immediately we want to do it. But the *Bhagavad-gītā* tells us that the meditator must learn to control the mind: "For one who has conquered the mind, then his mind is the best of friends; but for one who has failed to do so, his mind will be the greatest enemy."

The materialistic mind attempts to enjoy by employing the senses to experience matter and material relationships. It is full of unlimited ideas for sense gratification, and being perpetually restless, it constantly flickers from one sense object to another. In doing so, the mind vacillates between hankering for some material gain and lamenting some loss or frustration.

In the *Bhagavad-gītā* Kṛṣṇa explains, "One who is not in transcendental consciousness can have neither a controlled mind nor steady intelligence, without which there is no possibility of peace. And how can there be any happiness without peace?" By chanting the Hare Kṛṣṇa *mantra,* we can control the mind, instead of letting it control us.

Mantra is a Sanskrit word. *Man* means "mind," and *tra* means "to deliver." Thus, a *mantra* is a transcendental sound vibration with potency to liberate the mind from material conditioning.

In his commentary on *Śrīmad-Bhāgavatam,* Śrīla Prabhupāda explains, "Our entanglement in material affairs is begun from material sound." Each day we hear material sounds from radio and television, from friends and relatives, and based on what we hear, we act. But as Śrīla Prabhupāda points out, "There is sound in the spiritual world also. If we approach that sound, then our spiritual life begins." When we control the mind by focusing it on the purely spiritual sound vibration of the Hare Kṛṣṇa *mantra,* the mind becomes calm. As "music has charms to soothe a savage breast," so the spiritual sound of the *mantra* soothes the restless mind. The Hare Kṛṣṇa *mantra,* being imbued with God's own supreme energies, has the power to subdue all kinds of mental disturbance. Just as a reservoir of water is transparent when unagitated, our mental perceptions become clear and pure when the mind is no longer agitated by the waves of material desires. The mind in its pure state, like a mirror cleansed of dust, will then reflect undistorted images of reality, allowing us to go beneath the surface and perceive the essential spiritual quality of all life's experiences.

Knowledge of the Self

The *Vedas* state that consciousness is a symptom of the soul. In its pure condition, the soul exists in the spiritual world; but when it falls down into contact with matter, the living being is covered by an illusion called false egoism. False ego bewilders the consciousness, causing us to identify with our material bodies. But we are not our material body. When we look at our hand or leg, we say, "This is my hand" or "This is my leg." The conscious self, the "I," is therefore the owner and observer of the body. Intellectually, this fact is easily understandable, and by the spiritual realization that results from chanting, this truth can be directly and continuously experienced.

When the living being identifies with the material body and loses awareness of his real, spiritual self, he inevitably fears death, old age, and disease. He fears loss of beauty, intelligence, and strength and experiences countless other anxieties and false emotions relating to the temporary body. But by chanting, even in the early stages, we realize ourselves to be pure and changeless spirit souls, completely distinct from the material body. Because the *mantra* is a completely pure spiritual sound vibration, it has the power to restore our consciousness to its original, uncontaminated condition. At this point, we cease to be controlled by jealousy, bigotry, pride, envy, and hatred. As Lord Kṛṣṇa tells us in *Bhagavad-gītā,* the soul is "unborn, eternal, ever-existing, undying, and primeval." As our false bodily identification dissolves and we perceive our true transcendental existence, we automatically transcend all the fears and anxieties of material existence. We no longer think "I am American. I am Russian. I am black. I am white."

Attaining real self-awareness also gives us the ability to see the spiritual nature of all living beings. When our natural, spiritual feelings are awakened, we experience the ultimate unity of all life. This is what it means to become a liberated person; by spiritual realization we become free of all animosity and envy toward other living things.

This higher vision is explained by Śrīla Prabhupāda in the *Transcendental Teachings of Prahlāda Mahārāja.* "When a man becomes fully Kṛṣṇa conscious he does not see, 'Here is an animal, here is a cat, here is a dog, and here is a worm.' He sees everything as part and parcel of Kṛṣṇa. This is nicely explained in the *Bhagavad-gītā,* 'One who is actually learned in Kṛṣṇa consciousness becomes a lover of the universe.' Unless one is situated on the Kṛṣṇa conscious platform, there is no question of universal brotherhood."

Brings Real Happiness

Everyone is thirsting for true and lasting happiness. But because material pleasure is limited and temporary, it is compared to a tiny drop of moisture in the desert. It gives us no permanent relief, because material sensations and relationships lack the potency to satisfy the spiritual desires of the soul. But the chanting of Hare Kṛṣṇa provides complete satisfaction because it places us in direct contact with God and His spiritual pleasure potency. God is full of all bliss, and when we enter His association, we can also experience the same transcendental happiness.

In the Vedic literature there is an interesting account of how the pleasure of chanting far exceeds any material benefit. Once a poor *brāhmaṇa* priest worshiped the demigod Lord Siva for a material benediction. Lord Śiva, however, advised him to go to the sage Sanātana Gosvāmī to obtain his heart's desire. Upon learning that Sanātana Gosvāmī had a mystical stone capable of producing gold, the poor *brāhmaṇa* asked if he could have it. Sanatana consented and told the *brāhmaṇa* he could take the stone from its resting place in his garbage pile. The *brāhmaṇa* departed in great joy, for he could now get as much gold as he desired simply by touching the stone to iron. But afterward he thought, "If a touchstone is the best benediction, why did Sanātana Gosvāmī keep it with the garbage?"

He returned to Sanātana Gosvāmī to satisfy his curiosity. The sage then informed him, "Actually, this is not the best benediction. But are you prepared to take the best benediction from me?"

"Yes," the poor *brāhmaṇa* replied. "I have come to you for the best benediction." Sanātana Gosvāmī then told him to throw the touchstone in the water nearby and then return. The poor *brāhmaṇa* did so, and when he came back, the saintly Sanātana initiated him into the chanting of the Hare Kṛṣṇa *mantra,* the sublime method for experiencing the highest spiritual pleasure.

Liberation from Karma

The law of *karma* means that for every material action performed, nature forces an equivalent reaction upon the performer, or, as the Bible states, "As ye sow, so shall ye reap."

Material activities can be compared to seeds. Initially they are performed, or planted, and over the course of time they gradually fructify, releasing their resultant reactions. Enmeshed in this web of actions and reactions, we are forced to accept one material body after another to experience our karmic destiny. But freedom from *karma* is possible by sincere chanting of Kṛṣṇa's transcendental names. Since God's names are filled with transcendental energy, when the living being associates with the divine sound vibration, he is freed from the endless cycle of *karma.*

Just as seeds fried in a pan lose their potency to sprout, so karmic reactions are rendered impotent by the power of the holy names of God. Kṛṣṇa is like the sun. The sun is so powerful that it can purify whatever comes into contact with it. If any object enters the sun globe, it is immediately transformed into fire. Similarly, when our consciousness is absorbed in the transcendental sound of Krsna, His internal energies act to purify us of all karmic reactions. In his commentary on *Śrīmad-Bhāgavatam,* Śrīla Prabhupāda stresses, "The holy name is so spiritually potent that simply by chanting the holy name one can be freed from the reactions to all sinful activity."

Freedom from Reincarnation

The *Vedas* teach that the living entity, the soul, is eternal, but due to past activities and material desires, it perpetually accepts different material bodies. As long as we have material desires, nature, acting under God's direction, will award us one material body after another. This is called transmigration of the soul, or reincarnation. Actually, this changing of bodies is not surprising, because even in this life we go through many bodies. First we have the body of an infant, then a child, later an adult, and finally the form of an old man or woman. Similarly, after the passing of our old body, we get a new one.

Liberation from this cycle, known as *saṁsāra,* or the endless wheel of birth and death, is possible by freeing our consciousness from material desires. By chanting Hare Kṛṣṇa, we revive the natural spiritual desires of the soul. Just as the nature of the body is to be attracted to sense gratification, the nature of the soul is to be attracted to God. Chanting awakens our original God consciousness and our desire to serve and associate with Him. By this simple change in consciousness, we can transcend the cycle of reincarnation.

Śrīla Prabhupāda discusses this in his commentary on the *Bhagavad-gītā.* "The cumulative effect of the thoughts and actions of one's life influences one's thoughts at death; therefore the actions of this life determine one's future state of being. If one is transcendentally absorbed in Kṛṣṇa's service, then his next body will be trancendental [spiritual], not physical. Therefore the chanting of the Hare Kṛṣṇa *mantra* is the best process for successfully changing one's state of being to transcendental life."

The Ultimate Benefit—Love of God

The final goal and the highest fruit of chanting is complete God realization and pure love of God.

As our consciousness becomes increasingly purified, our steady spiritual advancement is reflected in our character and behavior. As the sun approaches the horizon, it is preceded by increasing warmth and illumination. Similarly, as realization of Kṛṣṇa's holy name is revived within the heart, this increasing spiritual awareness manifests in all aspects of our personality. Ultimately, the eternal, loving relationship between God and the living being is revived. Before entering the material world, each soul had a unique spiritual relationship with God. This loving relationship is thousands of times greater and more intense than any love experienced in the material world. This is described in the *Caitanya-caritāmṛta:* "Pure love for Kṛṣṇa is eternally established in the heart of living entities. It is not something to be gained from another source. When the heart is purified by hearing and chanting, the living entity is awakened."

In our eternal, constitutional position in the spiritual world, we are able to associate with God directly, serving Him in a spiritual form just suitable for our mood of love and devotion. In this relationship of spiritual love, the pure devotee is absorbed in transcendental ecstasy. This state of ecstasy is described in *The Nectar of Devotion.* "At that time one's heart becomes illuminated like the sun. The sun is far above the planetary systems, and there is no possibility of its being covered by any kind of cloud. Similarly, when a devotee is purified like the sun, from his heart there is a diffusion of ecstatic love more glorious than the sunshine."

There are no hard-and-fast rules for chanting Hare Kṛṣṇa. The most wonderful thing about *mantra* meditation is that one may chant anywhere and at any time.

9

Techniques for Chanting

The meditation business is flourishing these days. Modern-day "messiahs," "*gurus,*" and "incarnations," with all varieties of *mantras,* are quite common, as eager customers flock to the feet of self-styled saviors. One so-called *guru* instructs his disciples in supercharged techniques for becoming a financial success. Another tells his followers that meditation will make their intelligence sharper and the body more fit to enjoy sensual pleasures. Still other "*gurus*" claim that sex is the ultimate goal of life and that unlimited sex will free one from all material desires. Some chic spiritual seekers pay a lot of money for secret *mantras* that they believe will allow them to perform mystic feats. But the Vedic literatures issue stern warnings about charlatan *gurus* and bogus *mantras*.

If a person is actually serious about spiritual life, he or she must come in contact with a bona fide spiritual master and learn from him the science of Kṛṣṇa consciousness. The *Muṇḍaka Upaniṣad* states that "In order to learn the transcendental science, one must approach a bona fide spiritual master in disciplic succession, who is fixed in the Absolute Truth."

Not just any *guru* will do This verse informs us that the spiritual master must be in disciplic succession from Lord

Kṛṣṇa, the supreme spiritual master. Such a genuine spiritual master receives Kṛṣṇa's teachings through the disciplic chain and distributes them exactly as he has heard them from his spiritual master, without watering them down or altering them to suit his whims. A bona fide *guru* is not an impersonalist or voidist. He will never claim to be God; rather, he aspires to be a servant of God and His devotees. Such a *guru* is called *ācārya,* or one who teaches by example. His life is free from all material desires and sinful behavior, his character is exemplary, and he must be qualified to deliver his disciples from the path of repeated birth and death. The Kṛṣṇa conscious *guru* is absorbed in service to or meditation on the Supreme Lord at every moment.

Since the holy name of Kṛṣṇa is completely spiritual, it must be received from a pure representative or servant of Kṛṣṇa, who acts as a transparent via medium between God and the sincere spiritual seeker. *Mantras* received from any other type of "*guru*" simply will not work.

His Divine Grace A. C. Bhaktivedanta Swami Prabhupāda writes in the *Śrīmad-Bhāgavatam:* "Unless one follows the disciplic succession, the *mantra* one receives will be chanted for no purpose. Nowadays there are so many rascal *gurus* who manufacture their *mantras* as a process for material advancement, not for spiritual advancement. Still, the *mantra* cannot be successful if it is manufactured. *Mantras* and the process of devotional service have special power, provided they are received from the authorized person."

Receiving the Hare Kṛṣṇa *mantra* from a bona fide *guru* who is in complete harmony with Kṛṣṇa's teachings in the *Bhagavad-gītā* is the single most important aspect of chanting Hare Kṛṣṇa.

Chanting the Hare Kṛṣṇa *mahā-mantra* is the simplest of all processes of self-realization There are no exorbitant fees; the *mantra* is free. The thriving business of selling *mantras* is a form of cheating. The test of a person's sincerity is not that he pays some money but that he is willing to change his life.

In order to chant Hare Kṛṣṇa, one need not equip oneself with expensive props and paraphernalia, learn to stand on one's head, or perform other difficult postures or breathing exercises. The only equipment one needs is a tongue and ears. Everyone already has these. The tongue simply has to vibrate Kṛṣṇa's holy names, and the ears must hear it. By this simple process alone, one can achieve all perfection.

How to Chant

There are no hard-and-fast rules for chanting Hare Kṛṣṇa. The most wonderful thing about *mantra* meditation is that one may chant anywhere—at home or at work, driving in the car, or riding on the bus or subway. And one may chant at any time.

There are two basic types of chanting. Personal meditation, where one chants alone on beads, is called *japa*. When one chants in responsive fashion with others, this is called *kīrtana*. *Kīrtana* is usually accompanied by musical instruments and clapping. Both forms of chanting are recommended and beneficial.

To perform the first type of meditation, one needs only a set of *japa* beads. These may be purchased from any Hare Kṛṣṇa temple or by filling out the coupon in the back of this book. Or, if you like, you can make your own beads at home.

If you decide to make your *japa* beads, follow these simple instructions:

1. Buy 109 large round beads and some strong, thick nylon thread.

2. Tie a knot about six inches from the end of a long piece of the thread and then string the beads, tying a knot after each one.

3. After stringing 108 beads, pull the two ends of thread through one large master bead.

4. This bead is called the Kṛṣṇa bead. Tie a knot next to it and cut off the excess thread. You now have your own set of *japa* beads.

To meditate with the beads, hold them in your right hand. Hold the first bead with your thumb and middle finger (see illustration on page 110) and chant the complete *maha-mantra*—Hare Kṛṣṇa, Hare Kṛṣṇa, Kṛṣṇa Kṛṣṇa, Hare Hare/ Hare Rāma, Hare Rāma, Rāma Rāma, Hare Hare. Then go to the next bead, holding it with the same two fingers, again chanting the entire *mantra*. Then go on to the next bead and then the next, continuing in this way until you have chanted on all 108 beads and have come to the Kṛṣṇa bead. You have now completed one "round" of chanting. Do not chant on the Kṛṣṇa bead, but turn the beads around and chant on them in the opposite direction, one after another. Chanting on beads is especially helpful, for it engages the sense of touch in the meditative process and helps you concentrate even more on the sound of the *mantra*.

You may want to chant *japa* indoors, but you can chant just as comfortably walking along the beach or hiking in the mountains. Just bring your beads along with you. If you chant sitting down, you should assume a comfortable position (preferably not lying down or slouching, for there's always the tendency to fall asleep). You can chant as loudly or as softly as you like, but it's important to pronounce the *mantra* clearly and loudly enough to hear yourself. The mind may have a tendency to wander off to other matters when you chant, for the mind is flickering and unsteady, always looking for something new and pleasurable to absorb itself in. If your mind wanders (to anything except Kṛṣṇa and things related to Him), gently bring it back to the transcendental sound vibration. It won't be difficult, because the mind is easily satisfied when absorbed in the divine sound of the Lord's holy names (unlike other meditational practices, where one may be asked to fix one's mind on "nothing" or "the void").

One may chant *japa* at any time, but the Vedic literatures note that certain hours of the day are most auspicious for performing spiritual activities. The early morning hours just before and after sunrise are generally a time of stillness and quietude, excellently suited to contemplative chanting. Many people find it especially helpful to set aside a certain amount of time at the same time each day for chanting. Start with one or two rounds a day, and gradually increase the number until you reach sixteen, the recommended minimum for serious chanters.

While *japa* is a form of meditation involving you, your beads, and the Supreme Lord, *kīrtana,* on the other hand, is a form of group meditation, where one sings the *mantra*, sometimes accompanied by musical instruments. You may have seen a *kīrtana* party chanting on the streets of your city, for the devotees frequently perform this type of chanting to demonstrate the process and allow as many people as possible to benefit from hearing the holy names.

One may hold a *kīrtana* at home with family or friends, with one person leading the chanting and the others responding. *Kīrtana* is more of a supercharged meditational process, where in addition to hearing oneself chant, one also benefits by hearing the chanting of others. Musical instruments are nice, but not necessary. One may sing the *mantra* to any melody and clap one's hands. If you have children, they can sing along as well and make spiritual advancement. You can get the whole family together every evening for chanting.

The sounds of the material world are boring, hackneyed and monotonous, but chanting is an ever-increasingly refreshing experience. Make a test yourself. Try chanting some word or phrase for even five minutes. If you chant "Coca-Cola" over and over again, even for a few minutes, it becomes practically unbearable. There's no pleasure in it. But the sound of Kṛṣṇa's names is transcendental, and as one chants he wants to chant more and more.

Enhancing Your Chanting

Although one receives immense benefit however and whenever one may chant Hare Kṛṣṇa, the great spiritual masters who are authorities on chanting suggest that the practitioner employ certain practical techniques that will enhance the chanting and bring quicker results as well.

The more one chants, the more easily he will be able to follow the principles listed below, for as one chants, he gains spiritual strength and develops a higher taste. When one begins to relish spiritual pleasure from chanting, giving up bad habits that may hinder one's spiritual progress becomes much easier.

1. Just by chanting Hare Kṛṣṇa, one will automatically want to follow the four regulative principles of spiritual life:

   A. No eating of meat, fish, or eggs.
   B. No intoxication.
   C. No gambling.
   D. No illicit sex (sex outside of marriage or not meant for the procreation of God conscious children).

The four above-mentioned activities make it especially difficult for one to progress in spiritual life, because they increase one's attachment to material things. Therefore, they are not recommended for one who has taken up the chanting of Hare Kṛṣṇa. The chanting is so powerful, however, that one may begin chanting at any stage, and the chanting will help one to make the necessary adjustments.

2. One should regularly read the Vedic literatures, especially the *Bhagavad-gītā* and *Śrīmad-Bhāgavatam.* If one simply hears about God, His uncommon activities and transcendental pastimes, the dust accumulated in the heart due to long association with the material world will be cleansed. By regularly hearing about Kṛṣṇa and the spiritual world, where Kṛṣṇa enjoys eternal pastimes with His devotees, one will fully understand the nature of the soul, true spiritual activities, and the complete procedure for obtaining release from the material world.

3. In order to be more fully immunized against material contamination, one should eat only vegetarian foods that have been spiritualized by being offered to the Supreme Lord. There is a karmic reaction involved when one takes the life of any living being (including plants), but the Supreme Lord states in the *Gītā* that if one offers Him vegetarian foods, He will nullify that reaction.

4. One should offer the fruit of one's work to the Supreme Lord. When one works for his own pleasure or satisfaction, he must accept the karmic reactions to his activities, but if one dedicates his work to God and works only for His satisfaction, there is no karmic reaction. Work performed as service to the Lord not only frees one from karma, but awakens one's dormant love for Kṛṣṇa.

5. As much as possible, one who is serious about chanting Hare Kṛṣṇa should associate with other like-minded persons. This gives one great spiritual strength. Śrīla Prabhupāda formed the International Society for Krishna Consciousness so that persons who are sincere about

becoming conscious of God and their eternal loving relationship with Him may benefit from associating with others who are also on the path back home to the spiritual world.

Eventually, serious chanters will want to take initiation from a bona fide spiritual master. Initiation is recommended in the Vedic scriptures, for it dramatically helps one in chanting Hare Kṛṣṇa and assists in the awakening of our original spiritual consciousness. There are qualified spiritual masters in the International Society for Krishna Consciousness throughout the world who are willing to assist anyone sincere about becoming God conscious.

Śrīla Prabhupāda has indicated that those desirous of taking initiation must follow the regulative principles mentioned earlier and chant each day on beads a minimum of sixteen rounds. Śrī Caitanya Mahāprabhu, the incarnation of Kṛṣṇa who popularized the chanting of the holy names five hundred years ago in West Bengal, India, introduced the system of chanting a fixed number of rounds each day. Careful completion of sixteen rounds daily will help the disciple to remember Kṛṣṇa always.

That, in essence, is what Kṛṣṇa consciousness is all about—always remembering Kṛṣṇa and never forgetting Him. And chanting is the simplest way of maintaining this constant state of God consciousness, for the mystical potency contained in the *mantra's* vibration will always keep you in touch with God and your own original, spiritual nature. All of God's innumerable spiritual potencies, including His transcendental pleasure principle, are contained in His holy names. Therefore, the pleasure you will feel as you begin to chant will be far, far greater than any material happiness you have ever experienced. And the more you chant Hare Kṛṣṇa, the happier you will feel.

BOOKS by
His Divine Grace
A.C. Bhaktivedanta Swami Prabhupada

Bhagavad-gītā As It Is
Śrīmad-Bhāgavatam, Cantos 1-12 (18 volumes)
Śrī Caitanya-caritāmṛta (17 volumes)
Teachings of Lord Kapila, the Son of Devahūti
Teachings of Lord Caitanya
Teachings of Queen Kuntī
The Nectar of Devotion
The Science of Self-Realization
The Journey of Self-Discovery
Kṛṣṇa, the Supreme Personality of Godhead (2 vols)
The Nectar of Instruction
Śrī Īśopaniṣad
Easy Journey to Other Planets
Kṛṣṇa Consciousness: The Topmost Yoga System
Perfect Questions, Perfect Answers
Kṛṣṇa, the Reservoir of Pleasure
The Path of Perfection
Life Comes from Life
The Perfection of Yoga
Beyond Birth and Death
On the Way to Kṛṣṇa
Rājā-vidya: The King of Knowledge
Elevation to Kṛṣṇa Consciousness
Kṛṣṇa Consciousness: The Matchless Gift
Geetār-gan (Bengali)
Vairāgya-vidya (Bengali)
Buddhi-yoga (Bengali)
Bhakti-ratna-bolī (Bengali)
Back to Godhead magazine (founder)

All Bhaktivedanta Book Trust titles can be ordered through all good book shops and public libraries.

A complete catalog is available on request from:

The Bhaktivedanta Book Trust
P.O. Box 324
Borehamwood,
Herts.WD6 1NB,
U.K.

The Bhaktivedanta Book Trust
P.O. Box 262
Botany, NSW 2019
Australia

The Bhaktivedanta Book Trust
3764 Watseka Ave.
Los Angeles
CA 90034, U.S.A.

The International Society for Krishna Consciousness

Centers Around the World

Founder-Ācārya: His Divine Grace A. C. Bhaktivedanta Swami Prabhupāda

NORTH AMERICA

CANADA

Calgary, Alberta — 313 Fourth St. N.E., T2E 3S3/ Tel. (403) 238-0602
Edomonton, Alberta — 9353 35th Ave., TSE 5R5/ Tel. (403) 439-9999
Montreal, Quebec — 1626 Pie IX Boulevard, H1V 2C5/ Tel. (514) 521-1301
Ottawa, Ontario — 212 Somerset St. E., K1N 6V4/ Tel. (613) 565-6544
Regina, Saskatchewan — 1279 Retallack St., S4T 2H8/ Tel. (306) 525-1640
Toronto, Ontario — 243 Avenue Rd., M5R 2J6/ Tel. (416) 922-5415
Vancouver, B.C. — 5462 S.E. Marine Dr., Burnaby V5J 3G8/ Tel. (604) 433-9728
Victoria, B.C.—4020 Loyola St., V8N 4V4/ Tel. (604) 477-0557

FARM COMMUNITY

Ashcroft, B.C. — Saranagati Dhama, Box 99, V0K 1A0

U.S.A.

Atlanta, Georgia — 1287 South Ponce de Leon Ave. N.E., 30306/ Tel. (404) 378-9234
Baltimore, Maryland — 200 Bloomsbury Ave., Catonsville, 21228/ Tel. (410) 744-4069
Berkeley, California — 2334 Stuart St., 94705/ Tel. (510) 644-1113
Boise, Idaho — 1615 Martha St., 83706/ Tel. (208) 344-4274
Boston, Massachusetts — 72 Com-monwealth Ave., 02116/ Tel. (617) 247-8611
Chicago, Illinois — 1716 W. Lunt Ave., 60626/ Tel. (773) 973-0900
Columbus, Ohio — 379 W. Eighth Ave., 43201/ Tel. (614) 421-1661
Dallas, Texas — 5430 Gurley Ave., 75223/ Tel. (214) 827-6330
Denver, Colorado — 1400 Cherry St., 80220/ Tel. (303) 333-5461
Detroit, Michigan — 383 Lenox Ave., 48215/ Tel. (313) 824-6000
Gainesville, Florida — 214 N.W. 14th St., 32603/ Tel. (352) 336-4183
Gurabo, Puerto Rico — HC01-Box 8440 HC-01, 00778-9763/ Tel. (809) 737-1658
Hartford, Connecticut — 1683 Main St., E. Hartford, 06108/ Tel. (203) 289-7252
Honolulu, Hawaii — 51 Coelho Way, 96817/ Tel. (808) 595-3433
Houston, Texas — 1320 W. 34th St., 77018/ Tel. (713) 686-4482
Laguna Beach, California — 285 Legion St., 92651/ Tel. (714) 494-7029
Long Island, New York — 197 S. Ocean Ave., Freeport, 11520/ Tel. (516) 223-4909
Los Angeles, California — 3764 Watseka Ave., 90034/ Tel. (310) 836-2676
Miami, Florida — 3220 Virginia St., 33133 (mail: P.O. Box 337, Coconut Grove, FL 33233)/ Tel. (305) 442-7218
New Orleans, Louisiana — 2936 Esplanade Ave., 70119/ Tel. (504) 486-3583
New York City (Brooklyn) — 305 Schermerhorn St., Brooklyn, 11217/ Tel. (718) 855-6714
New York City (Manhattan) — 26 Second Avenue, 10003/ Tel. (212) 420-1130
Philadelphia, Pennsylvania — 41 West Allens Lane, 19119/ Tel. (215) 247-4600
Portland, Oregon — 5137 N.E. 42 Ave., 97218/ Tel. (503) 287-3252
St. Louis, Missouri — 3926 Lindell Blvd., 63108/ Tel. (314) 535-8085
San Diego, California — 1030 Grand Ave., Pacific Beach, 92109/ Tel. (619) 483-2500
San Francisco, California — 84 Carl St., 94117/ Tel. (415) 661-7320
San Francisco, California — 2334 Stuart St., Berkeley, 94705/Tel. (510) 540-9215
Seattle, Washington — 1420 228th Ave. S.E., Issaquah, 98027/ Tel. (206) 391-3293
Spanish Fork, Utah — KHQN Radio, 8628 South State St., 84660/ Tel. (801) 798-3559
Tallahassee, Florida — 1323 Nylic St. (mail: P.O. Box 20224, 32304)/ Tel. (904) 681-9258
Towaco, New Jersey — P.O. Box 109, 07082/ Tel. (201) 299-0970
Tucson, Arizona — 711 E. Blacklidge Dr., 85719/ Tel. (520) 792-0630
Washington, D.C. — 3200 Ivy Way, Harwood, MD 20776/ Tel. (301) 261-4493
Washington, D.C. — 10310 Oaklyn Dr., Potomac, MD 20854/ Tel. (301) 299-2100

FARM COMMUNITIES

Alachua, Florida (New Ramana-reti) — Box 819, 32616/ Tel. (904) 462-2017
Carriere, Mississippi (New Talavan) — 31492 Anner Road, 39426/ Tel. (601) 799-1354
Gurabo, Puerto Rico (New Govardhana Hill) — (contact ISKCON Gurabo)
Hillsborough, North Carolina (New Goloka) — 1032 Dimmocks Mill Rd., 27278/ Tel. (919) 732-6492
Mulberry, Tennessee (Murari-sevaka) — Rt. No. 1, Box 146-A, 37359/ Tel (615) 759-6888
Port Royal, Pennsylvania (Gita Nagari) — R.D. No. 1, Box 839, 17082/ Tel. (717) 527-4101

RESTAURANTS AND DINING

Boise, Idaho — Govinda's, 500 W. Main St., 83702/ Tel. (208) 338-9710
Eugene, Oregon — Govinda's Vegetarian Buffet, 270 W. 8th St., 97401/ Tel. (503) 686-3531
Fresono, California — Govinda's, 2373 E. Shaw, 93710/ Tel. (209) 225-1230
Gainesville, Florida — Radha's, 125 NW 23rd Ave., 32609/ Tel. (352) 376-9012

EUROPE

UNITED KINGDOM AND IRELAND

Belfast, Northern Ireland — 140 Upper Dunmurray Lane, BT17 OHE/ Tel. +44 (01232) 620530
Birmingham, England — 84 Stanmore Rd., Edgebaston, B16 9TB/ Tel. +44 (0121) 420-4999
Coventry, England — Sri Sri Radha Krishna Cultural Centre, Kingfield Rd., Radford (mail: 19 Gloucester St., CV1 3BZ)/ Tel. +44 (01203) 555420
Dublin, Ireland — 56 Dame St., Dublin 2/ Tel. +353 (01) 679-1306
Glasgow, Scotland — Karuna Bhavan, Bankhouse Rd., Lesmahagow, Lanarkshire ML11 0ES/ Tel. +44 (01555) 894790
Leicester, England — 21 Thoresby St., North Evington. Leicester LE5 4GU/ Tel. +44 (0116) 2762587 or 2367723
Liverpool, England — 114A Bold St., Liverpool L1 4HY/ Tel. +44 (0151) 708 9400
London, England (city) — 10 Soho St., London W1V 5DA/ Tel. +44 (0171) 4373662 (business hours), 4393606 (other times); Govinda's Restaurant: 4374928
London, England (country) — Bhaktivedanta Manor, Letchmore Heath, Watford, Hertfordshire WD2 8EP/ Tel. +44 (01923) 857244
London, England (south) — 42 Enmore Road, South Norwood, London SE25/ Tel. +44 (0181) 656-4296
Manchester, England — 20 Mayfield Rd., Whalley Range, Manchester M16 8FT/ Tel. +44 (0161) 2264416
Newcastle upon Tyne, England — 21 Leazes Park Rd., NE1 4PF/ Tel. +44 (0191) 2220150

FARM COMMUNITIES

County Wicklow, Ireland — Rathgorragh, Kiltegan/ Tel. +353 508 73305
Lisnaskea, Norhtern Ireland — Hare Krishna Island, BT92 (GN Lisnaskea, Co. Fremanagh/ Tel. +44 (03657) 21512
London, England — (contact Bhaktivedanta Manor)

RESTAURANT

Manchester, England — Krishna's, 20 Cyril St., Manchester 14/ Tel. +44 (0161) 226 965 (Krishna conscious programs are held regularly in more than twenty other cities in the U.K. For information, contact Bhaktivedanta Books Ltd., Reader Services Dept., P.O. Box 324, Borehamwood, Herts WD6 1NB/ Tel +44 [0181] 905 1244.)

GERMANY

Abentheuer — Bockingstr 8, 55767 Abentheuer/ Tel. +49 (06782) 6364
Berlin — Bhakti Yoga Center, Muskauer Str. 27, 10997 Berlin/ Tel. +49 (030) 618 9112
Flensburg — Neuhoerup 1, 24980 Hoerup/ Tel. +49 (04639) 73 36
Hamburg — Muehlenstr. 93, 25421 Pinneberg/ Tel. +49 (04101) 2 39 31
Heidelberg — Center for Vedic Studies, Kürfuersten-Anlage 5, 69115 Heidelberg (mail: P.O. Box 101726, 69007 Heidelberg)/ Tel. +49 (06221) 16 51 01
Köln — Taunusstr. 40, 51105 Köln/ Tel. +49 (0221) 830 37 78
Munich — Tal 38, 80331 Munchen/ Tel +49 (089) 29 23 17

Nuremberg — Bhakti Yoga Center, Kopernikusplatz 12, 90459 Nürnberg/ Tel. +49 (0911) 45 32 86
Weimar — Rothauserbergweg 6, 99425 Weimar/ Tel. +49 (03643) 5 95 48
Wiesbaden — Schiersteiner Strasse 6, 65187 Wiesbaden/ Tel. +49 (0611) 37 33 12

ITALY

Asti — Roatto, Frazione Valle Reale 20/ Tel. +39 (0141) 938406
Bergamo — Villaggio Hare Krishna, Via Galileo Galilei 41, 24040 Chignolo D'isola (BG)/ Tel. +39 (035) 490706
Bologna — Via Ramo Barchetta 2, 40010 Bentivoglio (BO)/ Tel. +39 (051) 863924
Catania — Via San Nicolo al Borgo 28, 95128 Catania, Sicily/ jTel. +39 (095) 522-252
Naples — Via Vesuvio, N33, Ercolano LNA7/ Tel. +39 (081) 739-0398
Rome — Nepi, Sri Gaura Mandala, Via Mazzanese Km. 0,700 (dalla Cassia uscita Calcata), Pian del Pavone (Viterbo)/ Tel. +39 (0761) 527038
Vicenza — Via Roma 9, 36020 Albettone (Vicenza)/ Tel. +39 (0444) 790573 or 790566

SWEDEN

Göthenburg — Hojdgatan 22, 431 36 Moelndal/ Tel. +46 (031) 879648
Grödinge — Korsnäs Gård, 14792 Grödinge/ Tel. +46 (8530) 29151
Karlstad — ISKCON, Box 5155, 650 05 Karlstadø
Lund — Bredg 28 ipg, 222 21/ Tel. +46 (046) 120413
Malmö — Hare Krishna Temple, Gustav Adolfs Torg 10 A, 211 39 Malmö/ Tel. +46 (040) 127181
Stockholm — Fridhemsgatan 22, 11240 Stockholm/ Tel. +46 (08) 6549 002
Uppsala — Nannaskolan sal F 3, Kungsgatan 22 (mail: Box 833, 751 08, Uppsala)/ Tel. +46 (018) 102924 or 509956

SWITZERLAND

Basel — Hammerstrasse 11, 4058 Basel/ Tel. +41 (061) 693 26 38
Bern — Marktgasse 7, 3011 Bern/ Tel. +41 (031) 312 38 25
Lugano — Via ai Grotti, 6862 Rancate (TI)/ Tel. +41 (091) 46 66 16
Zürich — Bergstrasse 54, 8030 Zürich/ Tel. +41 (1) 262-33-88
Zürich — Preyergrasse 16, 8001 Zürich/ Tel. +41 (1) 251-88-51

OTHER COUNTRIES

Amsterdam, The Netherlands — Van Hilligaertstraat 17, 1072 JX, Amsterdam/ Tel. +31 (020) 6751404
Antwerp, Belgium — Amerikalei 184, 2000 Antwerpen/ Tel. +32 (03) 237-0037
Athens, Greece — Methymnis 18, Kipseli, 11257 Athens/ Tel. +30 (01) 8658384
Barcelona, Spain — c/de L'Oblit 67, 08026 Barcelona/ Tel. +34 (93) 347-9933
Belgrade, Serbia — VVZ-Veda, Custendilska 17, 11000 Beograd/ Tel. +381 (11) 781-695
Budapest, Hungary — Hare Krishna Temple, Mariaremetei ut. 77, Budapest 1028 II/Tel. +36 (01) 1768774
Copenhagen, Denmark — Baunevej 23, 3400 Hillerød/ Tel. +45 42286446
Debrecen, Hungary — L. Hegyi Mihalyne, U62, Debrecen 4030/ Tel. +36 (052) 342-496
Iasi, Romania — Stradela Moara De Vint 72, 6600 Iasi
Kaunas, Lithuania — Savanoryu 37, Kaunas/ Tel. +370 (07) 222574
Lisbon, Portugal — Rua Fernao Lopes, 6, Cascais 2750 (mail: Apartado 2489, Lisbo 1112)/ Tel. +351 (011) 286 713
Madrid, Spain — Espíritu Santo 19, 28004 Madrid/ Tel. +34 (91) 521-3096
Málaga, Spain — Ctra. Alora, 3 int., 29140 Churriana/ Tel. +34 (952) 621038
Oslo, Norway — Senter for Krishnabevissthet, Skolestien 11, 0373 Oslo 3/ Tel. +47 (022) 494790
Paris, France — 31 Rue Jean Vacquier, 93160 Noisy le Grand/ Tel. +33 (01) 43043263
Porto, Portugal — Rua S. Miguel, 19 C.P. 4000 (mail: Apartado 4108, 4002 Porto Codex)/ Tel. +351 (02) 2005469
Prague, Czech Republic — Jilova 290, Prague 5-Zlicin 155 21/ Tel. +42 (02) 3021282 or 3021608
Rotterdam, The Netherlands — Braamberg 45, 2905 BK Capelle a/d Yssel./ Tel. +31 (010) 4580873
Santa Cruz de Tenerife, Spain — C/ Castillo, 44, 4°, Santa Cruz 38003,Tenerife/ Tel. +34 (922) 241035

Sarajevo, Bosnia-Herzegovina — Saburina 11, 71000 Sarajevo/ Tel. +381 (071) 531-154
Septon-Durbuy, Belgium — Chateau de Petite Somme, 6940 Septon-Durbuy/ Tel. +32 (086) 322926
Shyauliai, Lithuania — Vytauto 65a, 5408 Shyauliai/ Tel. +370 (014) 99323
Vienna, Austria — Center for Vedic Studies, Rosenackerstrasse 26, 1170 Vienna/ Tel. +43 (01) 222455830

AUSTRALASIA

AUSTRALIA

Adelaide — 227 Henley Beach Rd., Torrensville, S. A. 5031/ Tel. +61 (08) 234-1378
Brisbane — 95 Bank Rd., Graceville, Q.L.D. (mail: P.O. Box 83, Indooroopilly 4068)/ Tel. +61 (07) 379-5455
Canberra — P.O Box 1411, Canberra ACT 2060/ Tel. +61 (06) 290-1869
Melbourne — 197 Danks St., Albert Park, Victoria 3206 (mail: P.O. Box 125)/ Tel. +61 (03) 699-5122
Perth — 356 Murray St., Perth (mail: P.O. Box 102, Bayswater, W. A. 6053)/ Tel. +61 (09) 481-1114 or 370-1552 (evenings)
Sydney — 180 Falcon St., North Sydney, N.S.W. 2060 (mail: P. O. Box 459, Cammeray, N.S.W. 2062)/ Tel. +61 (02) 959-4558
Sydney — 3296 King St., Newtown 2042/ Tel. +61 (02) 550-6524

FARM COMMUNITIES

Bambra (New Nandagram) — Oak Hill, Dean's Marsh Rd., Bambra, VIC 3241/ Tel. +61 (052) 88-7383
Millfield, N.S.W. — New Gokula Farm, Lewis Lane (off Mt.View Rd. Millfield near Cessnock), N.S.W. (mail: P.O. Box 399, Cessnock 2325, N.S.W.)/ Tel. +61 (049) 98-1800
Murwillumbah (New Govardhana) — Tyalgum Rd., Eungella, via Murwillumbah N. S. W. 2484 (mail: P.O. Box 687)/ Tel. +61 (066) 72-6579

RESTAURANTS

Brisbane — Govinda's, 1st floor, 99 Elizabeth Street/ Tel. +61 (07) 210-0255
Melbourne — Crossways, Floor 1, 123 Swanston St., Melbourne, Victoria 3000/ Tel. +61 (03) 650-2939
Melbourne — Gopal's, 139 Swanston St., Melbourne, Victoria 3000/ Tel. +61 (03) 650-1578
Perth — Hare Krishna Food for Life, 200 William St., Northbridge, WA 6003/ Tel. +61 (09) 227-1684
Sydney — Govinda's Upstairs and Govinda's Take-Away, 112 Darlinghurst Rd., Darlinghurst, N.S.W. 2010/ Tel. +61 (02) 380-5162

NEW ZEALAND, FIJI, AND PAPUA NEW GUINEA

Christchurch, New Zealand — 83 Bealey Ave. (mail: P.O. Box 25-190 Christchurch)/ Tel. +64 (03) 3665-174
Labasa, Fiji — Delailabasa (mail: P.O. Box 133)/ Tel. +679 812912
Lautoka, Fiji — 5 Tavewa Ave. (mail: P.O. Box 125)/ Tel. +679 664112
Port Moresby, Papua New Guinea — Section 23, Lot 46, Gordonia St., Hohola (mail: P. O. Box 571, POM NCD)/ Tel. +675 259213
Rakiraki, Fiji — Rewasa, Rakiraki (mail: P.O. Box 204)/ Tel. +679 694243
Suva, Fiji — Nasinu 7½ miles (mail: P.O. Box 7315)/ Tel. +679 393599
Wellington, New Zealand — 60 Wade St., Wadestown, Wellington (mail: P.O. Box 2753, Wellington)/ Tel. +64 (04) 4720510

FARM COMMUNITY

Auckland, New Zealand (New Varshan) — Hwy. 18, Riverhead, next to Huapai Golf Course (mail: R.D. 2, Kumeu, Auckland)/ Tel. +64 (09) 4128075

RESTAURANTS

Auckland, New Zealand — Gopal's, Civic House (1st floor), 291 Queen St./ Tel. +64 (09) 3034885
Christchurch, New Zealand — Gopal's, 143 Worcester St./ Tel. +64 (03) 3667-035
Labasa, Fiji — Hare Krishna Restaurant, Naseakula Road/ Tel. +679 811364
Lautoka, Fiji — Gopal's, Corner of Yasawa St. and Naviti St./ Tel. +679 662990
Suva, Fiji — Gopal's, 18 Pratt St./ Tel. +679 314154

BHAGAVAD-GĪTĀ AS IT IS

The world's most popular edition of a timeless classic.

Throughout the ages, the world's greatest minds have turned to the *Bhagavad-gītā* for answers to life's perennial questions. Renowned as the jewel of India's spiritual wisdom, the *Gītā* summarizes the profound Vedic knowledge concerning man's essential nature, his environment, and ultimately his relationship with God. With more than fifty million copies sold in twenty languages, *Bhagavad-gītā As It Is,* by His Divine Grace A.C. Bhaktivedanta Swami Prabhupāda, is the most widely read edition of the *Gītā* in the world. It includes the original Sanskrit text, phonetic transliterations, word-for-word meanings, translation, elaborate commentary, and many full-color illustrations. (Pocket version: translation and commentary only.)

Pocket	Vinyl	Hard	Deluxe
$3.90	$8.50	$10.30	$18.00
BGS	BGV	BGH	BGD

IN USA ORDER TOLL FREE 1-800-927-4152

GREAT
VEGETARIAN DISHES

Featuring over 100 stunning full-color photos, this new book is for spiritually aware people who want the exquisite taste of Hare Krishna cooking without a lot of time in the kitchen. The 240 international recipes were tested and refined by world-famous Hare Krishna chef Kūrma dāsa.

240 recipes, 192 pages, coffee-table-size hardback
US: $19.95 #GVD

THE HARE KRISHNA BOOK OF
VEGETARIAN COOKING

A colorfully illustrated, practical cookbook that not only helps you prepare authentic Indian dishes at home but also teaches you about the ancient tradition behind India's world-famous vegetarian cuisine.

130 kitchen-tested recipes, 300 pages, hardback
US: $11.60 #HKVC